BRITISH CASUALTIES 104,000 (OFFICIAL)

Evening News

HAMILTON FYFE CAUGHT BY UHLANS

Daily Mail

GREAT WATERPLANE RACE

Mr. HAWKER FLIES 390 MILES in 7 HOURS

Evening News

Daily Mail

L. G.

M. G.

Northcliffe
NAPOLEON OF FLEET STREET

Lord Northcliffe, journalist and newspaper proprietor, 1865-1922

Northcliffe

NAPOLEON OF FLEET STREET

by

Harry J. Greenwall

LONDON

ALLAN WINGATE

Published by
Allan Wingate (Publishers) Ltd
12 Beauchamp Place, London S.W.3

© 1957 *by Allan Wingate (Publishers) Ltd*

Made and printed in Great Britain
by the Ditchling Press Ltd
Ditchling Hassocks, Sussex

First Impression September 1957

iv

CONTENTS

ACKNOWLEDGMENTS

The Publishers and the Author wish to express their gratitude to Lord Rothermere; to Mr Donald Naylor and Mr Jeffries as well as to other members of the staff of Associated Newspapers Ltd, for the help received in compiling many of the illustrations for this book.

The Author wishes to add a personal word of thanks to secretaries of the late Lord Northcliffe; to Miss Louise Owen; Mr Hannen Swaffer and others who have given him valuable assistance. Much gratitude is also due to the proprietors of *The Times* and *Punch* for permission to reproduce numerous photographs and cartoons.

ILLUSTRATIONS

To my fellow adventurers
in the Street of Adventure

FOREWORD

'I Come to Bury Caesar'

USUALLY two schools of thought appear directly a biography is published: one school deplores that a Life of So-and-So has been written. The other school thinks it a pity that the biographer was not franker, that so much that could have been said has not been said. In the present case, this writer was faced with some special difficulties because possibly never did any man receive so much crushing criticism and unbounded loyalty as Alfred Harmsworth, later Viscount Northcliffe. Many men owed their careers to the Chief, as he liked to be called, and it is natural that they should rigidly avoid any suggestion of ingratitude, but if these people thought more logically they might realise that if the Chief was indeed the Colossus they claim he was, the all-wise, all-seeing, then it would be their bounden duty to produce evidence that would help to paint a portrait which would preserve for posterity a picture of the man as they believed him to be.

A number of biographies of Lord Northcliffe have been published, but, according to the subject of this biography himself, many others were written; they were never published because they did not meet with the approval of the Chief. This matter I deal with more fully in a subsequent chapter, but what I wish to make clear at this point is that I have not written an 'anti-Northcliffe' book, as several people who worked for the Chief feared. Here there is no raking up of scandals, no washing of dirty linen, no mud-slinging. This is a book about Northcliffe and the times in which he lived, but once again I must write a warning: I do not 'praise with faint damns', as Beerbohm Tree claimed somebody did to him.

This book is purely and simply a record, and I trust a faithful mirror. Undoubtedly it was a tragedy that the Press Empire Northcliffe so laboriously built was split up so quickly. It may be the gods were kind, and Britain escaped dire peril through the early passing of this moulder of mass opinions, of which he was such an unsurpassed master. I do not offer an opinion; I merely produce the facts, place the evidence before you and leave you to judge for yourselves.

But this must be said at this stage: although North-cliffe ruled by fear, by putting the fear of the 'sack', of dismissal, of being cast out into outer darkness, into the souls of his employees, no newspaper proprietor was able to gather so much loyalty and, in many cases, real affection, as did Northcliffe. To say that all the men who feared him, loved him, would be absurd, of course. Most of the men who feared him did so because they feared for their jobs. They did not hate him; they were hypnotised by the Northcliffe legend, the tale of a man swift to reward and equally swift to punish. It was the gambling instinct, something of which lies deep down inside most men, which led them to work and produce, in many cases, good work while the dice were being shaken and their fates were at stake.

The men who loved Northcliffe, who wept when he died, were, many of them, those who had been threatened with dismissal, and, in some cases, actually dismissed, but the affection they bore him cannot be overlooked.

As the mental malady of Northcliffe progressed and his actions became more and more unpredictable, it was tragic that there were none who loved him sufficiently, or were sufficiently unafraid of him, to pull out the switches and save the tottering Colossus from a headlong fall. By pretending that all was well with this man, by tampering with the unrelenting machine for mass publicity that he had himself created, those who lurked in the Northcliffian shadows did poor service to their dear god.

It was remarked at the time, by one of the *Daily Mail* directors, that there was nothing dramatic about Northcliffe's death. A strange thing to say, because what could be more dramatic than the death of Northcliffe on the roof of another man's house? What a story he would have made of that!

In this biographical study of Northcliffe I am endeavouring to project a film against a backcloth woven out of material made from the period through which he himself strode so masterfully. Northcliffe's times were, I submit, indubitably attuned to his career. He was bold enough to strike a new note, yet if his luck had not held good, that note would have had no golden echo. It might have vibrated but would soon have died away. Nevertheless, luck or good fortune is not enough to explain the rise of the two Harmsworth brothers, Alfred and Harold; luck may come to any man, but he must seize the hair of the head of the goddess as she passes by.

Alfred Harmsworth founded a weekly publication called *Answers to Correspondents*. This was no stroke of genius; he had worked in 'snippet' journalism and his new paper lacked originality, but he had the *flair* to make the changes which brought success.

The launching of the *Daily Mail* was a logical sequence to the birth of *Answers*. Here was an idea, a sound idea, an idea built up on the providing of a daily newspaper for the board school child, who, in

1896, had just reached school-leaving age; but where luck stood in good stead to Alfred Harmsworth was at the point where, soon after the *Daily Mail* was started, the Boer War began, and there opened a period wherein the whole life of Britain began to undergo startling changes. Alfred Harmsworth, Viscount Northcliffe, reported that period. He may have been lucky to have had that period to report, but he had the genius not to let go of the hair of the elusive goddess. He held on tightly, held on until . . . but that is a story you must read for yourselves.

Towards the end of this work I have allowed my fancy free rein. I have played with ideas of what might have happened in and to England if Northcliffe had maintained his health and mental activities and, instead of dying in 1922 at the age of fifty-seven, he had lived until, well, say 1947; he would have been eighty-two. Clemenceau was fighting a great fight at that age.

What might have happened? Would we have 'done a Munich'? Would Northcliffe have tried to unseat Montgomery as he tried to thrust out Kitchener? Would Northcliffe have been a Messiah, or a menace? This I leave to your judgement at the close of your reading.

H.J.G.

IN the third week of June 1922, loungers on the terrace of the Royal Automobile Club in Pall Mall, London, noticed workmen on the roof of a tall house in Carlton Gardens. The men among the chimney-pots, it was said, had begun their labours at nightfall the previous evening and had worked all night. The workmen withdrew, their task finished. They left behind them a little wooden hut; one could see nothing much more than the outline of it over the green tree tops which line the broad gulley between Pall Mall and the Gardens beyond, but some members identified the hut-crowned house as the residence of the Duke of Devonshire, reported to be at Chatsworth. The Duke had given a neighbour permission to have this shed erected; the neighbour required quietness and air. The neighbour was Viscount Northcliffe, a man of strange whims and fancies as becomes an Irishman. He had in his time created a large Press Empire and had amassed an immense fortune in the process. Now he was out of his head and lay dying on another man's roof. Below him and all around him was the London whose doings his minions had reported at his behest. But in the wider world great events were now happening. In his native Ireland, for instance, there was a tumultuous upheaval: there was

heavy fighting in Dublin where the Four Courts had
just been blown up; but the man on the roof knew
nothing of these things. In Fleet Street, the core of his
Empire, his men were filling columns in the *Daily Mail*
he had created, but the Chief, an unwieldy mass of
flesh hanging loosely on his shrunken frame, lay un-
conscious of it, in a morphia-induced sleep. Sometimes
he came out of his stupor and a hand would grope for
a telephone. Sometimes in Carmelite House, headquarters of his Empire, a ghostly voice would give an
order, sometimes to be broken off before completed,
as if another hand had come between the Chief and
his courtiers.

London had for long been buzzing with rumours,
with denials and counter-rumours. This colossus, before
whom men trembled when his voice thundered, had
for so long been behaving strangely. First people spoke
of his eccentricity, then of his violence, his physical
attacks on employees and attendants. The stories
reached London from Germany, from France and
from Switzerland. What was happening? why so much
mystery? people were asking one another. The man
who had fought, as he said, so that truth should prevail, was himself now nothing but a peg on which were
hung the strangest tales.

When did the first signs of the gathering twilight
that cut Northcliffe off from his activities show themselves? Could his acts of violence which occurred
during his most active years be considered traceable
to his mental deterioration? One of the Northcliffe
biographers, Tom Clarke, mentions two particular
acts of violence; on one occasion the Chief jumped on
the hat of a visitor who had annoyed him, and on
another occasion he kicked the rear of a caller. Clarke
appends no date to these statements. Were they then

Alfred Harmsworth 1885, when he was twenty years of age

*Bleriot flies the Channel, July 25, 1909. He arrives at Victoria Station,
London, accompanied by Lord Northcliffe*

the doings of a madman or were they, more likely, merely the outward signs of a violent temper which other Irishmen besides Northcliffe have been known to possess?

The impulse to dismiss, to cast out, was a trait in Northcliffe's character which became accentuated as the Chief entered early middle-age, but there is little doubt that the acts of dismissal became far more noticeable as the mental malady grew worse. The frontispiece to Clarke's book is a one-line letter from his Chief: 'My dear Tom Clarke, fire Blank.' The letter is dated November 1920, a little less than two years before Northcliffe died.

Evidence of Northcliffe's strange behaviour undoubtedly came to the surface in 1917. It was plain then that for some time he had been suffering from megalomania, a *folie de grandeur*, and it showed up during the years of the First World War, when Northcliffe had the fixed idea that the Germans had marked him down and intended to kill him. This idea he expressed to a journalist, Sydney Moseley, in 1917. Northcliffe gave Moseley the information that he had that afternoon accepted the Cabinet's invitation to go to Washington as Special Envoy, and he added: 'I feel certain that the Germans will somehow get to know and there will be submarines lying in wait for me. They have tried hard enough, but still I'm taking a chance on it.'

Actually, there is no real evidence that there was or had ever been an attempt on his life. Sometimes German airplanes passed over the Kent coast, near his house at Elmwood, in Thanet, but no bombs were ever dropped.

Major-General Calwell wrote a biography of Field-Marshal Sir Henry Wilson wherein he said: 'During

January 1915, Wilson saw Northcliffe and found him
very bitter about the embargo on Press correspondents
at the front. "I could not get him to talk sense", said
Wilson. "He would not consider my offensive of the
two Sommes. At one moment he said the Boches were
on their last legs, in the next he said they had an
inexhaustible supply of men. He thought they were
starving because eels had gone up from four marks to
twenty-one marks! He agreed that Bucharest might
be taken, he agreed that Sweden would attack Russia,
that the long-range submarine was a real danger, and
said that Ireland would give any number of recruits if
there was a settlement, i.e. Home Rule? Berlin would
get hundreds of thousands of men then—and so on
and so on. Haig and Robertson were perfect, and had
now full power as he (Northcliffe) could 'force the
Government to do anything'!" '

Northcliffe said many times and to many people
that he would not live until the same age as his father.
Northcliffe was correct in his surmise; he died at the
age of fifty-seven.

During the first World War, Northcliffe made this
statement to Mr R. McNair Wilson in *The Times*
office: 'I'm told I'm suffering from heart disease. It
may not be true; I'm taking further advice and in
any case it does not matter, not much, at such times
as these. I think I shall be able to carry on, whatever
the verdict may be, until the war is won. I do want to
live long enough to see the end of the war, because I
think I may help a little.'

Northcliffe had undergone a minor throat operation
and had eye trouble.

These premonitions of an early death were repeated
constantly to members of his family and to members of
his staff, but there is no evidence of any medical

history which need have made him so morbidly inclined. Nevertheless, he was right.

Among the men who worked for Northcliffe in the early aftermath of World War No. 1 was an American journalist, the late Whythe Williams, who tells that in 1919 he thought he had found signs of Northcliffe's mental deterioration. Williams said that while he was representing the *Daily Mail* in Berlin, the German Foreign Office made him a present of three photostat copies of the original Treaty of Versailles, which at that moment had not been made public. Williams thought he had an important scoop, too long to cable, so he took a train to France and cabled Northcliffe, who sent a reply to Boulogne telling Williams to come at once to Elmwood. At Folkestone, Northcliffe's chauffeur, Pine, was waiting for him. When Williams reached Northcliffe's house, the Chief was in bed, but he had left orders for Williams to meet him in the library at seven the next morning.

Williams found Northcliffe talking to someone on the telephone; he was connected with *The Times* office in London. 'His (Northcliffe's) face was flushed and angry', says Williams. "What have you done with the moon?" he shouted. "I said the moon—the MOON." The shouts became louder. "Someone has moved the moon." A pause. "Well, if it is moved again, whoever does it is fired." He banged down the receiver and turned to me saying: "Good morning—sleep well?" as though he had seen me daily. He then peevishly explained that "some wretch in Printing House Square" had placed the weather report on a different page than usual.

'Again the telephone rang. Northcliffe seized it and bawled a "hello". Then his voice sank to a whisper: "You know, my dear, that the doctor forbids me to

B

speak. You should know better than to telephone."
Again he abruptly disconnected, saying to me: "That
was only my sister—now let's get to work".'

Williams put a copy of the Treaty on Northcliffe's
desk. Northcliffe picked it up very gingerly, glanced
at it a moment, then casually put it aside. 'Very
interesting', he said; 'very interesting indeed—something for our archives.'

Actually a version of the Treaty was pieced together,
and Northcliffe told Williams to take the article to
London. He sent him in his own car with instructions:
'After you have delivered the story, you sleep in my
bed in *The Times* office—the same bed that all the
Walters slept in for a hundred years.'

Williams returned to Elmwood for further instructions. He says he remembered Northcliffe's 'almost
child-like pleasure' in receiving gifts from members
of the staff, so he had picked up two small bronze medals
in Berlin and now handed Northcliffe the first one. It
was the souvenir medal commemorating the sinking of
the Lusitania. 'Northcliffe thanked me, but only
showed a mild interest. Northcliffe said that he could
not "swallow the statement that the medal had been
authorised by the German Government". He thought
it was a fake turned out during the Armistice.'

Then Williams handed over the second medal,
which was a caricature of Northcliffe himself spreading
incendiary ink all over the world.

'Had I turned over the Crown Jewels', said
Williams, 'he could not have shown greater joy.'
Northcliffe had his old mother staying with him, now
he shouted for her. 'Mother, oh mother, come quickly.
Come and see what Mr Williams brought me from
Berlin.' He then said to Williams: 'Really, I don't
know how to thank you. I have heard about this

medal, but could scarcely believe it. It is marvellous.'

Northcliffe and his mother examined the medal 'as though it was some precious metal'. All through luncheon Northcliffe talked about it and repeated his thanks. After the meal the Chief and the journalist paced the lawn. 'Do I pay you enough salary?' asked Northcliffe.

'Certainly not', replied Williams. Northcliffe again sent Williams in his car to London, but this time with a note to the *Daily Mail* Editor saying Williams' salary was to be increased by £500 a year! 'Not a bad return for a medal which cost a shilling', comments Williams.

Williams, however, never saw his Chief again. The American returned to Berlin and then went to Paris and soon afterwards he left the paper. Some of Northcliffe's sensational salary-raising efforts did end that way. Was he to blame? Did those who kept his money-bags think the Chief was too generous?

When indeed did the light really begin to fade and the twilight gather around the head of this restless genius?

The late Hamilton Fyfe, for so long associated with Northcliffe, dates the twilight period as beginning in 1917. Fyfe puts the change in Northcliffe as being due to 'a mystical belief that he was the man appointed to clear up the chaos into which the world had fallen'. Fyfe affirms that such change as he himself did not appear to notice prior to 1917 was in no way due to any vanity, although others, judges of character of equal calibre, are just as sure that Northcliffe was a vain man. John Buchan, the author (later Lord Tweedsmuir, Governor-General of Canada), wrote: 'Had he had more normal education and discipline he might have been a great man, for when unswayed by vanity he had sound judgment and a penetrating insight'.

Sir Julian Byng (Lord Byng of Vimy) wrote: 'He narrowly missed greatness, owing to instability of purpose born of mental impatience, approaching chronic fretfulness. He would take up a thing with enthusiasm and drop it as soon as interest evaporated.' Byng believed Northcliffe to be successful 'as long as the fever was on him'.

Indeed this moulder of mass suggestion had moments of penetrating insight which can be best viewed after the passing of time. When Douglas Fairbanks the elder and his then wife Mary Pickford paid their first visit to London and were received with delirious hysteria by Londoners, Northcliffe and Winston Churchill attended an afternoon reception the film couple held at the Ritz Hotel, Piccadilly. The two men stood at a window at the crowd milling up and down Constitution Hill. 'What does all this mean?' asked Churchill. 'I'll tell you in ten years time', replied Northcliffe.

Writing of Northcliffe's wartime mission to Washington, Fyfe says: 'Before he left the United States he (Northcliffe) was convinced that there was laid upon him a mission far greater than that of setting in order financial relations between the two Governments. He went back to London *prepared to receive an offer of the Premiership and resolved to accept it.*' The italics are mine.

Fyfe states in his biography that Northcliffe had no ambitions, but surely, to aspire to the Premiership of Great Britain is an ambition? If it is not, then of equal certainty such a thought must spring from vanity; vanity sometimes leads to megalomania, and megalomania may lead to insanity. Was Northcliffe insane, and if he was insane, when did he become so? Tom

Clarke refutes the suggestion that Northcliffe was insane, and says that when Mr Hannen Swaffer wrote that Northcliffe 'died mad' he was incorrect and should have known better, but is not this the expression of an opinion made by a loyal ex-employee (Clarke was once News Editor of the *Daily Mail*) rather than something submitted after weighing up all the evidence?

The late Sir Max Pemberton, a life-long friend of Northcliffe, said he asked one of his friends, who spent twenty-one years at Carmelite House, to give a sketch of the great journalist at work.

The journalist friend said that from his own observation he was inclined to give 1903 as the year when there were signs of the relaxing of the personal grip on the details of the paper (the *Daily Mail*). Pemberton's friend was reporting the Whitaker Wright trial. Northcliffe told the reporter that his work at the first day of the trial was 'unintelligible'. Every day afterwards the reporter spoke first and asked: 'Don't you think it is much clearer today?' Northcliffe smiled and answered 'Yes'. The writer commented that he was convinced that his proprietor had read neither the first report which he had criticised, nor the later ones which he had been invited to praise. This in 1903, only seven years after the *Daily Mail* was launched!

What was there to account for this 'relaxing of the personal grip'? If you accept the statements by several of Northcliffe's biographers, the Chief retained this grip until the end, but the Whitaker Wright trial was a tremendous sensation. When Wright was sentenced to five years penal servitude, he swallowed half a packet of cyanide of potassium and died, but Northcliffe, 'the great journalist', was believed to have never read a word of the reports!

What *can* one make of this? Was Northcliffe already entering the twilight period in which we now see him, dying on the roof of another man's house?

Sometimes while Northcliffe lay dying, his mind cleared, but even in this lonely retreat someone must have brought him news from the outer world; someone who told him of the reports of his insanity. Northcliffe reached for a telephone and, according to Tom Clarke, this dramatic message Northcliffe himself transmitted to Carmelite House: 'I hear they are saying I am mad. Send down the best reporter to get the story.' But no reporter was ever sent.

At this time the flow of the famous daily bulletins which Northcliffe had been in the habit of sending to the *Daily Mail* over a period of many years had ceased. The bulletins were sent by telephone by one of the Chief's secretaries early in the morning, usually after he had seen his own newspapers and his rivals when abroad. The bulletins were usually cabled. In the beginning it was customary for the bulletins to go to the Editor, but then the circle widened and copies were circulated among the various departments. As the mental malady progressed, the bulletins often contained insulting personal messages. Then came Northcliffe's instructions that a daily copy of the bulletin was to be given to the chief commissionaire in Carmelite House and he was ordered to show it 'to anybody who cared to see it'. During his lifetime Northcliffe issued between six and seven thousand of these *communiqués*, many of them too libellous for publication.

The bulletins did not always refer to newspaper matters; Northcliffe retained a number of private spies—'ferrets' he called them—and many of the bulletins referred to alleged discoveries by these 'ferrets'.

He lay there, listening to the chimes of nearby Big Ben and talking about them to his attendants. In moments of calmness and sanity he dictated notes to his mother.

He lay there, tossing and sweating and dropping off into the morphia-induced sleep. If physical suffering there had been, it had passed; but the mental suffering, what of that, for in the intervals of sanity there must have been such suffering? He had said, not long before he died, that he was a man without friends; that was a form of persecution mania which had played hide and seek with him during a great part of his life; that was a delusion. He had friends, affectionate and loving friends, but they could do nothing for him. The twilight was closing in and night was at hand.

What were the thoughts of this multi-millionaire? Did he repine, did he regret? The sure answer to that question we will never know. Perhaps he thought of the men he had made and unmade; as the Westminster chimes rang through his head he might well have remembered his early struggles, the battles he won, the strife and the pettiness and the fruits of victory turned to bitterness. Did he remember the women who had loved him and who had borne him children?

Of what did he think as the twilight turned into the night and the wings of Death flapped round the hut? On August 14, 1922, he died.

IN July 1865, when Alfred Harmsworth was born at Chapelizod on the outskirts of Dublin, many things of great importance were happening up and down the world. In North America Abraham Lincoln was assassinated, after being elected President for a second term of office. Then the Civil War ended, the same month that the great Lord Palmerston, Prime Minister of Great Britain, died. On the Continent of Europe there were ominous rumblings.

Alfred Harmsworth was the eldest child of fourteen brothers and sisters, and was named after his father, a barrister with few briefs who wrote unpaid articles for the Irish reviews. Mrs Harmsworth was a Miss Geraldine Maffett, a handsome woman of strong character. She was the daughter of an Ulster land agent who did some private banking on the side. She was twenty-nine when she married and her husband was one year her junior. Prior to her marriage, Mrs Harmsworth had travelled on the Continent, quite an unusual thing for young Irish ladies in the middle of the nineteenth century. Now she was married and might have looked forward to a reasonably peaceful life in Ireland, but when her first child was born the country was blazing with hate and anger of the English. The end of the Civil War across the Atlantic caused the Irish to believe that soon the Americans would come and help throw the English out of Ireland. Actually, although the power of the American Fenians was possibly greatly exaggerated, they were feared and their boast of raising and arming a quarter of a million men in Ireland was probably not entirely an idle one. In any case, the fear of the possibilities of 'the troubles' caused Mrs Harmsworth to think seriously of removing her little family to England.

Although she had the idea of leaving the country of her birth, the family had little money so Mrs Harmsworth persuaded her husband to begin to read for the English Bar. While he did so, she quietly went about her plans, hurried on no doubt by the increasing troubles close to the house and the rising flame of the Fenians.

It was when the baby Alfred was two years old that the flight to London took place. The family left the house by night, a house that Northcliffe eventually bought. The Harmsworth family went to live in Rose Cottage, close to the pond in the Vale of Health, Hampstead Heath.

In later life, Northcliffe would boast that he could remember every detail of the night flight from Dublin to London; his memory was good, but it is not likely that events which happened at the age of two would be mentally photographed and retained. More likely Mrs Harmsworth helped memory as she helped in other directions to mould the mind and character of the son for whom of all her children she retained until his death the greatest affection. She was a good mother and he a very good son.

Although the events which they had left behind them continued to be the supreme interest of Mr and Mrs Harmsworth, they found that in England there

was less interest in Ireland and more in the rising
power of the King of Prussia. In the year the
Harmsworths settled in Hampstead, Prussia had
annexed a part of Denmark and the French were
possibly the next in line to be challenged by Prussia,
since Austria had succumbed.

England was divided in her sympathies; the German
influence at the English Court, with the exception of
the case of Albert Edward, Prince of Wales, swung a
part of England to the side of Prussia. The Harmsworths sided with Prussia, because the Fenians had
found support in France. It would seem, therefore,
that the Ulsterwoman and the English barrister still
had their hearts in Ireland.

Every morning Alfred Harmsworth the elder would
walk from his Hampstead cottage to his rooms in the
Temple, rooms later purchased by Alfred Harmsworth
the younger and maintained as a sort of family shrine.
Materially, matters now prospered better for the
father of the future Viscount Northcliffe. He became
one of the counsel for the Great Northern Railway. A
daughter and another son were born and at Rose
Cottage there were gatherings of writers and artists,
such as frequented Hampstead in those days.

The future Viscount Northcliffe could neither read
nor write until he was seven years of age. At the age of
five he attended a school kept by a Miss Budd, in
Priory Road, Kilburn. It is on record that the young
Harmsworth was a bright child with a very observant
mind, but the suggestion that a Mr Jealous, a friend
of Harmsworth senior, through a present of a small
box of printers' type on his seventh birthday caused
the future Napoleon of the Press to turn his mind to
newspapers, seems a little far-fetched.

The boy was taken away from Miss Budd's and

sent to a boarding school at Stamford in Lincolnshire,
a school for which he maintained a life-long hatred
due chiefly to the canings he received there. As counsel
for the Great Northern Railway, Harmsworth senior
was able to obtain free railway passes; on one occasion
his son Alfred enjoyed a ride on the footplate of a
locomotive from King's Cross, London, to Grantham,
in Lincolnshire. Undoubtedly the boy retained a vivid
recollection of this unorthodox journey and was to
talk of it all his life. Indeed, it is probable that this trip
planted the seed of interest in speed and locomotion
which never left him. He had no mechanical sense
whatsoever, but his concern with motoring and flying
was very real.

The Harmsworth family now moved to St John's
Wood, and young Alfred Harmsworth was entered as
a scholar at Henley House School, not very far from
Miss Budd's. The Headmaster, the Reverend Milne,
was the father of A. A. Milne, who became a
famous author. The young chemistry master, who
used to poke the fire with a fencing stick, also
became a world-famous author. He was Mr H. G.
Wells.

Henley House School was the cradle of young
Harmsworth's journalistic ambitions. He made little
headway with his studies; his knowledge of Latin and
Greek was nil, his history weak. At his Lincolnshire
school he had played Rugby football and had earned
the nickname of 'Dodger', but at his London school he
neglected games in order to indulge his wholehearted
enthusiasm for the printed word. In the Henley House
school magazine, young Harmsworth was able to give
his ideas a free rein; he wrote for it and in the end he
edited it. Among the things he wrote was a poem about
the joys of living in Hampstead. It was bad poetry,

written in 1882, when the author was seventeen; he
had already left school.

From the point of view of this budding journalist,
however, what was more important to him than the
writing of verse or notes in a school magazine was the
fact that he had the free run of a printing establish-
ment in Kilburn where the magazine was produced.
Here he was able to learn to set type, to make experiments which quite possibly stood him in good stead in
later life.

Harmsworth the elder, who had looked on his eldest
son's journalistic efforts with smiling tolerance, was,
nevertheless, in the words of the Queen who then sat
on the Throne of England, not amused: he consulted
his journalist friends who unanimously opposed the
idea of Alfred Harmsworth the younger becoming a
journalist. When the boy himself put his case to the
same people he received the same answer. Notwithstanding, he became a journalist.

His first job was reporting for the *Hampstead and
Highgate Express*, whose editor was the man Jealous,
the same who had given him a present of a box of type
on his seventh birthday.

The job, ill-paid as such jobs were, was not a success.
Alfred Harmsworth, as we will now call him, left it
and became a tutor. It is indeed a mystery how a lad of
such slight learning was able to secure such a post. The
family at home was increasing yearly, so the little
money Harmsworth earned was useful. He threw up
tutoring when a friend of his father's took him on a
European tour which lasted several months.

When he returned to London his father and mother
wanted to send him to a university, but the young man
refused. In later days he gave this reason: 'I was
against it at the time because I knew it would mean a

pinch for the others, and I did not think that would be fair. I wanted to help them as soon as I could, rather than to be a burden on them. But I have often regretted that I had to renounce what could have been of immense value to me . . . think of the social value of having been at a university! It is like being able to ride. Every young man who wants to get on should be able to ride—and to talk French.' Later he announced to someone else that to be a successful foreign correspondent a man should be able to ride a horse and wear a monocle. One of his young men took the statement very literally, and stayed a lifetime with the *Daily Mail*. His name is G. Ward Price.

That little triangle that jutted into St John's Wood with its base on High Road, Kilburn, contained the homes of many who became known in the literary, musical and theatrical world. Israel Zangwill lived there, and so did Max Pemberton. Achenberg, the famous music publisher, had a house inside the base of the triangle, a few doors from a family called Tripp whose daughter later danced her way to fame under the name of 'June'.

It was a sleepy, drowsy but pleasant neighbourhood where in springtime the front gardens were full of golden yellow and pale mauve laburnum blossom and sweet-smelling mayflowers. On May Day, 'Jack-in-the-Green' danced, and buxom milkmaids carried pails of frothy milk slung from their shoulders. In July the hot pavements were littered with the already dried-up leaves, and in the autumn the blue-coated Breton onion men hawked their wares from door to door. The only discordant noises were the pipe of the Punch and Judy man, the sharp bark of Dog Toby, and the occasional blare of a strolling German band. Indeed, the cries of this part of suburban London did little to disturb the drowsy peace; perhaps it was too drowsy for Alfred Harmsworth, whose soul demanded changes.

While studying the life of Viscount Northcliffe, I have read all the books of which he formed the subject and most of the many which make short or long references to him. Side by side with Northcliffe's statement concerning the abandonment of a university career, I came across what Sir Max Pemberton, who first knew Harmsworth in 1879, when they were neighbours, had to say about this university business: '. . . I spent my days with him for some years afterwards, until, in fact, I went to Cambridge, and he, who greatly desired to go, was caught up in the mesh of the journalistic net. . . .' These apparent contradictions are confusing, but I think that the confusion arises not from any fault of the biographers as much as from the changing statements made by Northcliffe himself. Pemberton writes of an impression gained at a time when he was in daily contact with his friend, whereas the other reports conversations which took place years later and retells Northcliffe's opinion of a period at a university not as an aid to education, but as a springboard for social advancement. As a cross-section of a mind which was destined to shape the opinions of the masses, this point is not without its importance.

Pemberton gives an interesting impression of Alfred Harmsworth, whom he met in St John's Wood when both were riding bicycles—not the smooth-riding machines of today, but the ancient penny-farthings, which had a fifty-two-inch wheel in front and a nineteen-inch wheel at the back! On their hard solid tyres the two boys, later with Alfred's younger brother Harold (the first Lord Rothermere), had lots of fun. Between long bicycle rides and playing the piano by ear, Alfred Harmsworth would scribble things and put them away, but now he was back from the European tour and he had to go to work in earnest.

Alfred Harmsworth started calling on editors and showing them his cuttings from the Henley House school magazine. According to Hamilton Fyfe, the proprietor of a number of weekly publications, Mr William Ingram, gave him a job at 11s. 6d. a week as assistant editor on one of his publications called *Youth*. Alfred Harmsworth eked out his income by writing occasional articles on cricket for the *Daily Telegraph*. Then he joined his editor Edward Morton in rooms in the Temple. Here he began to work in very hard earnest, doing social 'pars' for *Vanity Fair* and stories for a boys' paper called *Young Folks*. When he still lived at home he would go to his office attired in a morning coat and a top hat, but once he left home he became less formal and wore no hat at all.

Now came a blow. Harmsworth's father fell ill and money was needed at home, but his salary as assistant editor and the income from infrequent paragraphs was not sufficient. Harmsworth was seventeen; many years later, on January 30, 1922, eight months before he died, Harmsworth made an oblique reference to his experiences. Entered in his diary on the date mentioned is a quotation from a book, *Daily Light on the Daily Path*, which his mother gave him on the eve of his world tour. The quotation is: 'It is good for a man that he bear the yoke in his youth'. Northcliffe's comment on this is: 'I do often ask whether that my early success may not have spoiled me; but I did bear some yoke, a good deal more, in fact, than I like to talk about'. It was in the 'yoke' stage of his life that young Harmsworth went to visit George Augustus Sala, then the star writer of the *Daily*

Telegraph. Harmsworth wanted advice; Sala advised him to get out of journalism.

Harmsworth lost his job with *Youth* and for a period shared diggings with Max Pemberton, first in St John's Wood and later in Hampstead. One would have thought perhaps that as his mother required financial help in the home, her eldest son would have lived with her. 'I do not know how much Harmsworth earned by his pen in 1883, his eighteenth year, but I fancy it was not a very large sum', said R. McNair Wilson, who adds: 'I do know that he lived frugally, denying himself all luxury, and imposing on himself an iron discipline. I know, too, that he drove himself mercilessly to work.'

Writing of the same period, Sir Max Pemberton offers us this version: 'I will not say that at that period the Alfred Harmsworth whom I knew was that miracle of energy and action with which later years have made me familiar. . . . The volcano, I think, was on fire at its depths, but nothing came from it but a little smoke and a flame to remind those about him of its existence.' Pemberton says that Harmsworth's leading articles at this period were paid for at the rate of half-a-guinea a column. Certainly Sir Max mentions no 'yoke'; indeed he writes: '. . . our hands being often idle, we spent long hours upon Hampstead Heath or the tennis court. . . .'

It was at this period, however, that there came a change in Harmsworth's fortunes. Pemberton came down from Cambridge and met Harmsworth by accident. Harmsworth was most fashionably dressed. Photographs of him at this period show him to have been a very handsome youth. Those who knew him say his hair was golden; some say his eyes were blue, others green. He was tall and muscular. He already wore the red polka-dot ties to which he clung all his life.

The two friends, Harmsworth and Pemberton, went to try to sell articles to George Newnes, the owner and editor of a successful green-covered weekly paper called *Tit-Bits*. Newnes bought an article and the two young men became regular contributors. One day when they called, they were received by a short-sighted spectacled man of about Harmsworth's age who had obtained his job with Newnes because he had won a *Tit-Bits* competition which offered a job at £100 a year. The short-sighted young man was Arthur Pearson, later Sir Arthur Pearson, and destined to become Harmsworth's greatest rival in the newspaper field. Of the first meeting Pearson wrote: 'I can recall those manuscripts quite clearly. Both were written on ruled copy-book paper. One in very distinctive handwriting, not too legible, was called "Some Curious Butterflies" and its author was Alfred Harmsworth.'

Harmsworth, while still contributing to *Tit-Bits* and despising but studying this publication, took up a job at Coventry with Iliffe's and edited a bicycling weekly. His interest in cycling was unabated and, on one occasion, he rode from Bristol to London in the pouring rain and without any food. The result was pneumonia.

Harmsworth held the Coventry post for two years and resigned even though he had been offered a partnership. During the Coventry period he wrote a series of handbooks for Newnes, of the 'how-to-do-it' kind. One of these handbooks professed to teach betting people how to make money by backing horses. Harmsworth knew nothing of the sport of kings and was never at any time interested in it in the slightest degree.

C

When he returned to London, Harmsworth was twenty. He had been looking for a backer to advance him money to launch a paper. He had saved a little money himself, but he was not going to risk it. He met an Irish school-fellow named Carr and with him took a small office in Paternoster Square, London, from whence he intended to launch a paper—when he found a backer. He traded as Carr & Co. However, instead of a backer, Harmsworth found a wife.

He married a Miss Mary Milner, a childhood friend, the daughter of a West Indian planter. Of the future Lady Northcliffe, it was said: '. . . her nature was so sincere, her heart so warm, her feelings so spontaneous and her sense of humour so strong that she could never simulate, never seem to be other than she was, a woman of delightfully vivid intelligence and sparkling charm.'

The young married Harmsworth continued to look for a backer. A barrister who knew his father, a man named Edward Markwick who wrote occasional leaders for the *Daily Telegraph*, had invested a little money of his own in Carr & Co. Harmsworth had successfully negotiated the publication in England of an American magazine called *Outing*. More money was now required, so Markwick invested money belonging to his sister, but still more money was required; where could he obtain it?

The clue to the germ of the idea now in the mind of Alfred Harmsworth may be found in the statement he made to Sir Max Pemberton. Harmsworth believed that he had found the reason why George Newnes was making such a success. 'The board schools', said Harmsworth, 'are turning out hundreds and thousands of boys and girls annually who are anxious to read. They do not care for the ordinary newspaper. They have no interest in Society (here he was quite wrong), but they will read anything which is simple and is sufficiently interesting. The man who has produced this *Tit-Bits* has got hold of a bigger thing than he imagines. He is only at the very beginning of a development which is going to change the whole face of journalism. I shall try to get in with him. We could start one of these papers for a couple of thousand pounds, and we ought to be able to find the money. At any rate, I am going to make the attempt.' However, it was Pemberton and not Harmsworth who made the attempt.

Pemberton approached his father, a Mincing Lane merchant, but was rebuffed. Pemberton then sought out Lady Meux, of the brewery family. Lady Meux was 'sold' on the idea, but the family lawyer vetoed the investment. Neither did Harmsworth 'get in' with Newnes, except as an occasional contributor.

At this time there was working on the *Daily Telegraph* a Mr J. Hall Richardson who knew Edward Markwick. Markwick told Richardson that a new weekly periodical was about to appear in which he was interested; would Richardson meet a friend in Markwick's chambers?

Mr Richardson wrote: 'Certainly if I had had £500 when Alfred Harmsworth, at the crisis of his fortunes, asked me to join with him and a sleeping partner, known to me only by the name of the "Captain", I should have had a share of the business he was then founding. But I had neither the money nor the inclination to put it into his hands. Moreover, he found it elsewhere, largely because a particular lady was interested in his career.' Before writing of the mysterious lady we will explain the 'Captain'.

The obsequious Edward Markwick had an acquaintance, a retired sea captain named Beaumont, who since he left the sea had acquired an interest in a furrier's business. At the instance of Harmsworth, Markwick went scurrying off to Italy to find Beaumont and to persuade him to invest some money in the new weekly periodical. Markwick was successful in his quest, but how much did he obtain?

I understand Captain Beaumont invested £3,000. But who was the lady interested in Alfred Harmsworth's career? Alfred Harmsworth was a very handsome young man; all his life the ladies were kind to him, and it was neither the first time nor the last time that a lady became interested in the career of a handsome young man. Did not Henry Irving, the actor acquaintance of Northcliffe, find a lady backer in the person of the Baroness Burdett Coutts? Was not the young Harmsworth an infinitely better-looking young man than the actor? But to the question, who the lady was who became the 'angel' in the case of Alfred Harmsworth, I am afraid I must acknowledge my incompetence to give a satisfactory reply.

Harmsworth had worked for a while on the staff of the *Lady's Pictorial*, where he discovered how easily people—particularly women—bared their souls to editors and asked for advice. Harmsworth had the idea of producing a weekly paper devoted entirely to answering correspondents. He published his paper, *Answers to Correspondents*, in June 1888. There was absolutely nothing original about it; a paper with the same idea, called *The Oracle*, was already appearing. Neither was the general lay-out original; it was an imitation of *Tit-Bits*, but *Tit-Bits* had a green cover and *Answers to Correspondents* had an orange cover.

It was soon found, however, that the paper was largely faked. Many of the questions were so obviously framed in order to introduce articles which appeared soon afterwards. The make-up was heavy. The paper did not prove a success, but it provided the future Lord Northcliffe with the opportunity of displaying his genius as a promoter of a certain kind of reading matter.

Many years before Harmsworth's weekly was launched, there had been a sensational murder in Mersham Tunnel, on the London-to-Brighton line. Mr J. Hall Richardson specialised in crime reporting for the *Daily Telegraph*, and had in his possession the full story of the murderer from a man named Leroy. 'Will you let me have the story?' Harmsworth asked Richardson, who refused. But Harmsworth persuaded Richardson to write a two-column article and to loan for publication a letter from Leroy. To Richardson's astonishment, when his article was published, instead of receiving a fee, the paper announced he had won a prize of one guinea! According to Richardson, Harmsworth also retained the Leroy letter and Richardson says he had difficulty in getting it returned to him.

There was now another crisis in the affairs of Alfred Harmsworth; *Answers to Correspondents* was a failure! What could he do? Harmsworth lopped off the last two words of the title, brightened the make-up, making the paper easier to read, and then made the best *coup* in his whole career; he induced his brother Harold to join him.

Harold Harmsworth, second in the male line to Alfred, was three years his junior. He had also attended Henley House School, where it was said he had a head for figures. The future first Lord Rother-mere shared his elder brother's liking for cycling, but in no other way did he show signs of sharing Alfred's interests. On leaving school, Harold entered the mercantile marine branch of the Board of Trade; when Alfred was in difficulties with *Answers* Harold held a safe but not particularly well-paid job. Harold did not jump, as the saying is, at his brother's offer; he thought it over. Then he consented and Alfred never had a better moment of fortune throughout his life.

When Alfred beckoned to Harold, it looked as if the money invested by the mysterious lady, the sea captain, the barrister and barrister's sister, might well disappear down the drain, but the financial genius of Harold turned a loss in 1888 into a profit of £2,000 in October 1889.

Answers moved to Fleet Street, where Alfred Harmsworth began to think of competitions, once again copying *Tit-Bits*. In those days the British people liked to gamble, just as they do now, but there were no dogs, no football pools. People could have a 'three-penny up and down-er' on a horse, otherwise there were no outlets for the gambling instinct other than the competitions with cash prizes. For instance, Harmsworth bought a £52-a-year annuity—'FIFTY POUNDS A YEAR FOR LIFE'—and gave it to the reader who made the guess nearest to the actual amount of bullion in the vaults of the Bank of England on a certain date. Circulation leapt for ever upwards, but the authorities stepped in and stopped another similar prize award.

There were clever articles and serials, as well as prizes. 'Convict 99' set all England talking, and the phrase became part of the English language. A reporter called 'Mr Answers' did all sorts of interesting things, such as climbing a church steeple and going down in a diving-bell. This may sound very naïve these days, but throughout the ages readers have sought escape from reality and Alfred Harmsworth provided it. He was a fellow of infinite zest who never forgot what it was like to be a schoolboy; he provided light fare for those others who cherished nostalgic memories of school days. Some of Northcliffe's biographers stress his so-called schoolboy teasing humour, but some of this humour was undoubtedly of an unpleasant nature, as we shall see as we follow his subsequent career.

When the profits of *Answers* was many thousands a year, the Fleet Street office was fairly full of Harms-worth brothers. Harmsworth *père et mère* bred them and brother Alfred gave them jobs.

Napoleon Bonaparte made his brothers kings; Northcliffe, Napoleon of the Press, made his brothers rich men, and early in his career began to give them jobs, but from the very beginning these younger brothers were the butts of jokes.

Very soon after the foundation of the *Daily Mail*, the period to which we are now moving, Alfred Harms-worth imported an American stunt artist named Charles Balch. At the same time he singled out for favouritism a young reporter just down from Cam-bridge, and invited him to his house in Berkeley Square; there he fed him with rich foods and plied him with compliments. His young friend was destined for high honours; the young man mentioned the names of the giants in Carmelite House. Harmsworth snapped his fingers at those names. They were pretty good, he said, but nothing compared to what his young friend would become if he did as his Chief told him.

The next morning he was early at the office; too excited to wait for the lift, he bounded upstairs, taking two steps in his stride. On the first floor he collided with the Chief. 'Who the devil are you, bumping into me like that?' thundered Harmsworth.

'W-h-hy, I'm Blank who dined with you last night', stammered the unhappy young man. 'Nonsense!' barked Harmsworth. 'Never seen you before in my life!'

The unfortunate Blank wandered on to the reporters' room where he met Balch, who said: 'Say, young man, you look pretty down in the mouth; what's bitten you?'

Blank told his story. Balch commented: 'You should have said to him: "Say, Chief, don't you recognise me? I'm one of your brothers!"'

In 1889, the youth of Britain was regaled with a penny illustrated weekly called *Ally Sloper's Half Holiday*. Alfred Harmsworth copied that and gave youth a halfpenny comic called *Comic Cuts*. Then he gave the girls *Forget-me-Not* and began to throw off weeklies just as a tomato plant throws off budding fruit. As a sidelight on the mentality of the masses for whom the Harmsworth brothers were catering, it may be said that soon *Comic Cuts* was showing a profit of £25,000 a year!

Within two years the firm was making a profit exceeding £100,000 a year, thanks largely to Harold's genius as a financier.

It was at this period in his life that the subject of this biography purchased a small estate in the Isle of Thanet called Elmwood. Alfred Harmsworth had long since learned to appreciate the wonderful air of the island, an island in theory only, and as Elmwood was Northcliffe's favourite home where he drafted most of his plans, a description of it is germane to this narrative.

Elmwood, in the fair county of Kent, played a large part in Northcliffe's life; not only was it the favourite of the many homes and houses he purchased during his tempestuous career, but from the nearby hamlet, Northcliffe, he took his title.

Alfred Harmsworth first went to live close to the shore of Thanet because doctors had prescribed rest and fresh air. It had the advantage of being less than seventy miles from London—not too far from Fleet Street. Certainly it possessed all one understands by the meaning of that peaceful word 'rest', and as for the fresh air, is it not legendary among the natives of this region that the air blows straight from the North Pole?

When young Harmsworth first went to live at Elmwood, between the lighthouse of North Foreland and the quaint little village of Reading Street, the countryside around Elmwood was typical of the England which lay in a drowsy stupor until the trumpet of the newspaper Colossus caused it to awake.

There were no motor-cars to stir the dust of the Kentish lanes; maybe the summer days then were no hotter than the summer days now, but looking back, summers seem to have been just a long-drawn-out chain of cloudless days and warm starry nights, when a breeze just rippled the softly lapping sea.

Close to Elmwood, just within pleasant walking distance, was the little seaside resort of Broadstairs— Broadstairs with the Dickensian air.

Dickens had once lived there, but even if one had not known that, one expected to meet Miss Trotwood —or Mr Micawber himself, humming an air and twirling his cane as he watched the fishing-boats from Broadstairs' black wooden jetty.

Two hours in a charabanc took you to Canterbury, or to Pegwell Bay, at the mouth of the Stour, so famous for its shrimps. And the Waterloo Tea Garden, queen of the many bosky gardens where they gave you

strong tea in thick dark brown tea-pots, and what piles
of bread and butter and home-made jam and fresh
lettuce! The coy little cottages with tall glass jars in
the windows, where you walked between the towering
hollyhocks to purchase a 'pennorth of bulls'-eyes'.

The roaring sands of Margate Town; the Hall-by-
the-Sea belonging to 'Lord' George Sanger, whose
circus was a product of Kent. The pierrots and Uncle
Bones' Minstrels, the black-faced entertainers. The
band on the 'Fort' where around the bandstand the
children barn-danced.

Ah, me! The languorous evenings when the moon
silvered the sea and the Band of the Royal Marines
(from Walmer) played selections from the London
musical comedies.

The blazing summer days when one watched the
paddle steamer *La Marguerite* en route from Tilbury
to Boulogne; the *Conqueror*, which paddled her way to
nearby Ramsgate, with an occasional maritime jaunt
around the Goodwin Sands. Once again, it was
peaceful unspoilt England into which the impetuous,
tumultuous Harmsworth thrust his way.

Harmsworth as such, and later as Lord Northcliffe,
did many things to Elmwood. Across the way from
him lived Mr Harry Marks, proprietor of the *Financial
Times*, M.P. for Thanet, a constituency later repre-
sented by Alfred's nephew, Esmond Harmsworth, the
present Lord Rothermere. Marks lived in an ugly
house called Callis Court. Elmwood had charm, despite
what Northcliffe did to it. In the garden he built a
model of a Canadian farmhouse; to the house he added
a billiard room, reputedly so that his chauffeur Pine
could play billiards with his private golf 'pro', Sandy
Thompson. Pine drove Northcliffe all his life but
Northcliffe had a signed letter from Pine, agreeing

that in case of an accident 'it's all my fault'. There
never was an accident.

In the garden was a bungalow in which Northcliffe
worked. There was a piano in the bungalow, but
Northcliffe, who played by ear, was never heard to
perform on the instrument. There were files of foreign
publications to which Northcliffe would turn for
inspiration, meaning in common parlance to see
whether there was anything worth lifting.

Hanging on one wall of the bungalow was a blackboard, ruled off with the names of his various publications, and when an idea occurred to him he would
inscribe it in its appropriate column. There was also
a space for general ideas.

As telephoning became more and more a part of
every-day life, Elmwood was fitted with inter-com-
munication apparatus from room to room and an
elaborate system of direct lines to the offices of his
publications, but the house never lost its charm.

Although an addict of early rising for others, Alfred
Harmsworth during the pioneer days of his life himself
never rose until such a time when, as he said, 'the day
was well aired'. He liked sea water, but not sea bathing,
and used to have the gardeners carry pails of sea water
from the beach to be heated for his morning bath.
The gardeners were dismissed when the Chief discovered that they, in order to avoid the toiling climb
from the beach, were drawing water from the garden
lily-pond and adding a little local colour with the aid
of seaweed.

While the new weeklies were appearing with
rapidity and mostly with success, Alfred paid his first
visit to New York. Joseph Pulitzer at that time owned
the New York *World*; he allowed young Harmsworth
to edit his newspaper for one night 'to show them how

it should be done', as Sir Max Pemberton so naïvely
wrote. But Pemberton does not relate that Pulitzer
understood 'stunts' very well, and every notable
visiting British journalist was invited to edit his newspaper, for one night only. When Arthur Pearson paid
his first visit to New York, he also received this
invitation, and like Harmsworth, accepted it. Incidentally, both Joseph Pulitzer and Arthur Pearson
died blinded men.

Back in again London, where Pearson had now left
Newnes' and had launched a periodical entitled
Pearson's Weekly, also in the competition game, and
where other publications were challenging with
mediocre success the long lead established by the
Harmsworth brothers, Alfred began to look for wider
pastures which could be cultivated. He had made up
his mind that the *Answers* technique could be applied
to a daily newspaper.

In 1894, the London evening newspapers did not
number a single 'popular' paper amongst them. Today
there are only three evening newspapers in London,
the world's largest city, but in 1894 there existed the
Star, *Sun*, *Evening Standard*, *Evening News*, *Pall Mall
Gazette*, *Globe*, and *Westminster Gazette*.

Each and every one of these publications made an
appeal to what was called the 'upper classes', meaning
really the educated people. The London evening
newspapers of the day—all of them appearing with
green or rose tinted newsprint—had a very distinct
literary flavour, but not one, with the possible
exception of the *Star*, which featured horse-racing,
made any attempt to appeal to the hundreds of
thousands of Londoners who had learned to read and
write at the board schools. These people and their
fellows in the provinces were being journalistically

exploited by Harmsworth's weeklies, and they were now ripe as potential readers of a daily newspaper which would take the trouble to interest them. To launch a newspaper required immense capital, but once again the Goddess Luck trailed her locks before Alfred Harmsworth's eyes and he seized her tresses—with the aid of brother Harold.

The *Evening News* was in low financial water. It was the hey-day of Liberalism in Britain, and the *Evening News* was an organ of the Conservative Party which had sunk £300,000 in the venture. It seemed as if deep-sea divers would be required if ever the Party was going to recover a penny of its money.

The *Sun* was edited by T. P. O'Connor, M.P., who had as his assistant an impecunious Glasgow Irishman named Kennedy Jones, a brilliant journalist who was looking for a better job. Jones had acquired, by reason of some freakish wager, 12,000 worthless shares in the *Evening News*. Jones used his holding to secure a fortnight's option to purchase the paper. When the option —which Jones obtained at a meeting of creditors— had almost expired, he still had nobody in mind to whom he could sell his option.

The *Sun* offices were close to Harmsworth's office and Jones was used to seeing Alfred Harmsworth, immaculately dressed, driving up in a hansom cab, jumping out and dashing upstairs, the picture of bounding success. One afternoon, after the *Sun* had gone to press, Kennedy Jones stood moodily staring out of a window, when his eyes once again saw the familiar cab and fare. This time an idea flashed into his mind.

Instead of going to Harmsworth himself, Jones sent a young reporter named Louis Tracy to tell Alfred Harmsworth that he could buy the *Evening News*, lock, stock and barrel, for £25,000—one year's profits on *Comic Cuts*. Tracy did not disclose the name of his principal, but Harold Harmsworth drew the name from him. 'Go and fetch Kennedy Jones', he was told.

Jones arrived, a little nervous, but he began to say what he would do with the paper if he had it. Alfred was impressed, but Harold wanted more and more details. Finally Jones blurted out: 'I don't want any money for my option; you buy the paper and make me editor.'

After several days of investigations, the deal was closed. Under Harold Harmsworth's fantastic magical financial control, the *Evening News* became a paying proposition from the start. At the end of its first year in the possession of Alfred Harmsworth, the *Evening News* was showing a profit of £14,000!

On the editorial side of the paper there were clashes of opinion between Alfred Harmsworth and Kennedy Jones. 'Alf' (Jones, to the great dislike of Harmsworth, called him 'Alf'), said Kennedy Jones, 'seemed to think that the stuff he put in *Answers*, piffling little articles about Beau Brummell and Mary Queen of Scots, would please readers of a daily, but Crime was our game.' A big murder story came along, with mystery and a woman in it, and the *Evening News* sales leapt. Yes, Crime was, and is, the fare of the London evening newspapers, but actually both men were right. Alfred Harmsworth, the genius who promoted news, sensed that the *Answers* technique could, slightly changed, be applied to London evening journalism. Whether Kennedy Jones learned anything from Alfred Harmsworth is doubtful, but the notes made on the blackboard in the bungalow at Elmwood showed that Harmsworth was learning a lot from

'K.J.', as Kennedy Jones was known in the Street of Ink.

'K.J.' was a humanist and a man of the people. The late John Raphael told me this little story. One morning Raphael was in 'K.J.'s' office in Carmelite House, when a printer came in, showed 'K.J.' some proofs and went out again. 'That man', said 'K.J.', 'is my brother. He could do my job, but I'm damned if I could do his!'

The late Wickham Steed told this story about Alfred Harmsworth and the *Evening News* which may account for the future Lord Northcliffe's 'Jew-baiting', as Mr Tom Clarke calls it. Indeed, this incident may well have been the genesis of it.

'He (Alfred Harmsworth) had instructed his sub-editors to brighten the paper inexpensively by re-printing jokes and satirical paragraphs from American comic papers. One such paragraph referred to a mythical Jew on Broadway, who was supposed to have condoled with another Jew upon a disastrous fire in his premises last week and to have expressed the hope that the premises were insured.

' "Not last week, you fool, next week!" was the alleged rejoinder.

'As ill-luck would have it, a Jewish tradesman in Shoreditch, bearing the same name as that given to the mythical Jew in the American paper, had claimed insurance for a fire in his London premises. He promptly issued a writ for libel against the *Evening News*. In vain did Harmsworth protest that he was totally unaware of the British Jew's name and of the fact that the premises in Shoreditch had been burned. He had either to run the risk of a libel action or to compensate the plaintiff in cash. Harmsworth chose the latter course and paid £600 indemnity—where-

upon he received a grateful letter from the British
Jew, who told him that a small syndicate which had
been formed to run the action against the *Evening
News* would be giving a little dinner party to celebrate
its triumph; it would be very happy if Mr Alfred
Harmsworth would attend it!'

While Alfred Harmsworth was learning from
Kennedy Jones, other influences began to form an
imprint on his character. The Harmsworths, as
Hamilton Fyfe points out, had German relatives, so
it was perfectly natural that Alfred Harmsworth
should be interested in Germany. Mr McNair Wilson
claims that Alfred Harmsworth spoke German, but
that is not so; Alfred Harmsworth could not speak any
foreign language; his interest in Germany at this
period—1895—centred mainly around the Kaiser
Wilhelm, whom Alfred Harmsworth thought a very
great man. There were two Englishmen whose words
at this period began to deeply impress Alfred; one was
Cecil Rhodes, of whom Britain was beginning to hear;
the other was Joseph Chamberlain, the former
Radical-Republican Mayor of Birmingham, but now
one of the leaders of the Tory Opposition to the Liberal
Lord Rosebery's Government.

The year 1895 was a turning point in Alfred Harmsworth's life and career. The Kiel Canal was opened;
the educated people in Britain began to take notice.
'Joe' Chamberlain, as he was now being called, began
to preach Imperialism. One of the first immediate
results was the defeat of the Rosebery Government, on
a matter of the shortage of high explosives—cordite,
to be precise. Lord Salisbury became Premier, 'Joe'
Chamberlain was his Colonial Secretary.

Alfred Harmsworth and the *Evening News* came out
strongly for Chamberlain; Alfred was a hundred per

cent Chamberlain man. He himself contested Portsmouth in the Unionist interest in the General Election
which followed Salisbury's appointment. The Union-
ists won the election, but Alfred Harmsworth was
beaten at Portsmouth. He returned to Fleet Street and
for ever afterwards 'distrusted all politicians'. Never
mind whether the grapes were sour, the fiasco at
Portsmouth changed the face of British journalism and
indirectly made Harold Harmsworth, at one period,
the richest man in the United Kingdom.

From Fleet Street, Alfred Harmsworth went to
Elmwood and, in the bungalow there, wrote items on
the blackboard; he wrote the things Kennedy Jones
had taught him, and he added notes of his own. The
fever was on him.

He was going to launch the *Daily Mail*.

D

WHEN the *Daily Mail* was founded by Alfred Harmsworth in 1896, British income tax was a few pence in the pound. Those calm and pleasant days one can now look back upon with a certain melancholy regret.

How much did it cost Harmsworth to launch the *Daily Mail*? Mr Wickham Steed, at one time Editor of *The Times* and for some years previous to North-cliffe's death in the closest touch with the Chief, quotes an unnamed source as affirming that Alfred Harmsworth spent 'less than £15,000' on his venture, which, he adds, made a profit from the start. Mr Bernard Falk, who was Editor of the *Weekly Dispatch* (now the *Sunday Dispatch*), the seventh-day companion to the *Daily Mail*, mentions the same figure, but Mr Hamilton Fyfe says £13,000 was the figure. The *Golden Jubilee Book of the Daily Mail*, however, says most explicitly, writing of the actual launching of the paper: 'For months then the Fleet Street loungers had heard stories of mysterious nightly activities at No. 2 Carmelite Street, where, by all accounts, a kind of phantom newspaper had been produced, a newspaper nobody saw. Every night for eleven weeks a whole staff had gone to work there and brought out a news-paper which never left the building. Rehearsal runs, they were called, and this period of trial production was known to have cost the Harmsworths at least £40,000.' But it must be said that the same publication affirms that 'the total initial capital was less than £15,000'. It would seem, however, that even fifty years ago, one could not start a London daily newspaper with a capital of only £15,000.

The Harmsworth idea was to produce a penny paper for a halfpenny; to give a new generation of readers the same 'advantages' that were accruing to the readers of the penny newspapers for fifty per cent less. The *Daily Mail* saw the light for the first time on May 4, 1896, and was essentially a Londoner's newspaper. What sort of a London was it that the future Lord Northcliffe sought to enlighten?

Londoners were reading in the mornings *The Times*, the *Daily Telegraph*, the *Standard*, the *Morning Post*, *Daily Chronicle*, *Daily News*, and the *Morning Advertiser*. In the previous chapter I dealt with the evening newspapers, but neither in the morning nor the evening was there much for the 'popular' taste. Thanks to Harmsworth and Pearson there were the bright weeklies devised for the New Generation; for the 'slavies', the domestic servants who spent most of their lives in the basements of the gaunt Victorian houses, there was the popular *Family Herald Supplement*, which published weekly instalments of novels about 'high life' for those below stairs, proving Harmsworth to be wrong in his *dicta* about the lack of interest in 'Society'.

Of course, there was *Punch* for the educated classes, with a short-lived rival called *Judy*. A weekly favourite was *Pick-Me-Up*, but for monthly reading for the educated, there was the green-covered *Strand* and a pink-covered magazine called *The Idler*, edited by a man who had made such a hit with *Three Men in a Boat*—Jerome K. Jerome.

The theatre at the time Alfred Harmsworth and his brother Harold, ably seconded by Kennedy Jones, launched the *Daily Mail*, had no rivals. There were just the musical comedy theatres, the comedy and the drama houses and the music-halls. One knew where one was, so to speak. Maybe there was nothing vitally exciting, but a man coming home from the Colonies knew what just to expect.

At the Gaiety Theatre in the Strand, the 'sacred lamp of burlesque' lit by Mr John Hollinsworth had gone out, but Mr George Edwardes was staging a series of *Girl* shows—*The Shop Girl*, *My Girl*, *The Runaway Girl*, *The Circus Girl*, and so forth. The cast was always the same and always good.

At the nearby Lyceum, Mr Henry Irving—the first actor to be knighted—was playing drama with Miss Ellen Terry; at the St James's Theatre, Mr George Alexander and Mrs Patrick Campbell were wringing tears with *The Second Mrs Tanqueray*.

Stalls cost half a guinea, dress circle seven and sixpence, upper boxes four shillings, pit two and six-pence and the gallery a shilling. There was no orderly queueing; when the doors opened there was a wild rush.

At the Savoy Mr Gilbert was still not speaking to Mr Sullivan, but their combined light operas were the joy of London. Was it for the frequenters of the London theatres, perhaps for those who paid their bob to be among 'the gods', that Harmsworth produced his paper? Was it for the theatre-goers in the suburbs?—for in those days each suburb had its very own theatre, where the bill was changed weekly.

Was the *Daily Mail* produced for the frequenters of

the music-hall, where the fare, there as everywhere else, was stable?

At the Tivoli, the Pavilion and the Oxford there were Marie Lloyd, Dan Leno, Lottie Collins, Herbert Campbell, Vesta Tilley, R. G. Knowles, Vesta Victoria, G. H. Chirgwin ('the White-Eyed Kaffir'), Cissie Loftus, top and bottom of the bill; each star singing three songs and dashing off in a private victoria or brougham from one hall to another. Was it for the music-hall audiences that the *Daily Mail* was produced? Anticipating by many years the wiles of a popular football pool promoter, Arthur Pearson did manage to make the American comedian Knowles advertise his 'Missing Word' competition. Harmsworth did not use the music-hall stage to help promote his publications, although, maybe *malgré lui*, the *Daily Mail* was advertised from the stage.

A popular comedian named Ernest Shand sang a song entitled: 'By kind permission of the *Daily Mail*'. 'Joe' Chamberlain was the public idol of the moment and Shand sang a song, a snatch from the chorus of which was: 'While we've Joseph, corn in Egypt will never fail'—

> 'He's a statesman and a brick, too
> 'And what he says he'll stick to
> 'By kind permission of the *Daily Mail*.'

Later, in a musical comedy called *Lady Madcap* at the Prince of Wales Theatre, a *soubrette* sang a song called 'Nerves', a quotation being:

> 'Nerves, nerves, nerves
> 'It isn't always true, but it serves,
> . . . .
> 'When *The Times* gets to threepence
> 'And the *Daily Mail*
> 'Gets on your nerves!'

The man who wrote the libretto of *Lady Madcap* was Lieut.-Col. Newnham-Davies, the 'Dwarf of Blood' of the *Sporting Times*, the famed *Pink 'Un*, the weekly theatrical-sporting paper beloved of the mashers, the 'Stage-Door Johnnies' whose spiritual home was Romano's in the Strand. Was it for them that the *Daily Mail* was published?

London may have been dull, viewed in retrospect, but there was nevertheless plenty of amusement. There were the Sunday League Excursions (to Brighton and back for 2s. 6d.); there were the summer evenings at Earl's Court Gardens, military bands and refreshments, the Water Chute. There was the River, Eel Pie Island, Tagg's Island, Boulter's Lock on Ascot Sunday when all the chestnut trees in Bushey Park were 'out'. People knew 'as sure as eggs are eggs', as they said, that Marie Lloyd would be in the Christmas pantomime at the Crown Theatre, Peckham, just as they knew that Dan Leno and Herbert Campbell would be in the 'Lane panto', when the Drury Lane autumn melodrama, by Cecil Raleigh *always*, ended its run.

There it was, gas-lit London, the pubs open to midnight, roaring roysterers rollicking homewards, hiccupping snatches from the chorus of some bawling baritone they had heard earlier in the evening. The sentiments were bathetic, of the 'Give my love to Mother, tell her how I love her' sort and fiercely patriotic in their effusions:

'When we say that England's master
'Remember who has made her so;
'It's the soldiers of the Queen, my lads. . . .'

Neither was the Navy left out, as this sample shows:
'Sons of the Sea
'All British born; sailing every Ocean
'Laughing foes to scorn

'They may build the ships, me lads
'And think they know the game
'But you can't beat the boys of the bulldog breed
'Who made Old England's name.'

Was it for these people that the *Daily Mail* was published? 'Trumpeter, what are you sounding now?' Alfred Harmsworth might have asked in effect, and the answer could come back: 'Britons will be Britons'.

Alfred Harmsworth had two heroes, twin Imperialists, Joseph Chamberlain and Cecil Rhodes. Harmsworth 'played them up'. Indeed, he 'played up' Rhodes so well that it led to the first spot of trouble into which the *Daily Mail* ran.

All the London newspapers were trying to obtain interviews with Rhodes and not one succeeded. Alfred Harmsworth, chief proprietor of the newspaper, decided to be his own reporter. He had not far to go; from Carmelite Street to De Keyser's Hotel was but a step. Rhodes would receive no one; nevertheless, Harmsworth went on up to Rhodes' rooms; no one at home, apparently, but Harmsworth heard splashings within. He investigated. Rhodes was sitting in a bath.

Rhodes, not unnaturally, was furious, but Harmsworth, unruffled, went on talking. With his observant eyes, he noticed that Rhodes was unable to reach the middle of his back, so he leaned over, as one Colossus to another, picked up the loofah and calmly washed the middle of the 'Empire Builder's' back!

Rhodes' 'sales-resistance' was broken down, and Harmsworth once again obtained what he wanted; trouble, however, was to come.

There was a reporter on the *Daily Mail* named Turnbull, who in earlier life had been a prize-fighter. Harmsworth, who had picked up many ideas in New York, had engaged as News Editor of the *Daily Mail* an

American-born Englishman, the late R. D. Blumen-
feld, who afterwards became Editor of the *Daily
Express*. Blumenfeld had previously been London
Correspondent of Mr Gordon Bennett's New York
Herald. Alfred Harmsworth met Blumenfeld in a Fleet
Street barber's shop and engaged him. The News
Editor had known Turnbull in New York; when
Harmsworth wanted another Cecil Rhodes story,
Blumenfeld sent Turnbull to get it.

Blumenfeld, who later became famed in British and
American journalistic annals as 'R.D.B.', records that
Turnbull purloined a secret document from Rhodes'
desk. Rhodes complained to Harmsworth. One of
Northcliffe's biographers writes that Alfred Harmsworth 'always left unpleasant duties to others'; in this
case Harmsworth sent Blumenfeld to try to appease
Rhodes. Blumenfeld's account of the meeting shows
the human side of Rhodes' character. He wanted to
know the nature of Turnbull's punishment; would he
be dismissed; if so, could be obtain another post?
Unfortunately, Mr Blumenfeld did not tell us whether
Turnbull was or was not dismissed, but he does say
that 'around 1902' Turnbull committed suicide.

What did the *Daily Mail* find to interest its readers
in those early days?

In point of fact, just as George Newnes had,
according to Alfred Harmsworth, started with *Tit-
Bits*, something bigger than he himself knew, so had
Harmsworth with the *Daily Mail* unleashed a tremendous force of potential mass thought-control. The
people of Britain did not know, it is more than
probable that British statesmen did not know, that
British Imperialism of which the *Daily Mail* was the
trumpet was about to touch its nadir. A sharp down-
ward curve loomed near, although the view of it was

hidden by a thick mist, a smoke-screen of traditional belief based on a long series of successful and victorious far-away Imperial wars. Such large tracts of school geography maps were coloured red, the colour of our Imperialism. Now here was Joseph Chamberlain standing out as the Apostle of it all.

Joseph Chamberlain, the ex-Radical, was arranging for Queen Victoria's Diamond Jubilee, one year after the foundation of the *Daily Mail*. It was to be a pageant of British Imperialism. Troops were to come from the farthest parts of 'the far-flung Empire' to march in procession through the strees of London, the 'heart of the Empire'.

Harmsworth not only pulled out all the stops of his morning and evening newspapers, but he used his weekly publications to strum the Imperial harp. *Answers*, the pioneer of the group which now numbered approximately three score of weeklies, published an exciting serial, a tale of an imaginary invasion of England while all the overseas troops were encamped in Britain waiting to take part in the Jubilee procession. Actually, Harmsworth had already used a similar idea. In 1895, the year he unsuccessfully contested Portsmouth in the Unionist interest, he had purchased a local newspaper wherein he ran a serial entitled 'The Siege of Portsmouth'. Harmsworth had a liking for such stories. Years after, when Mr Haldane, the Secretary of State for War, formed the Territorial Army, Harmsworth (Lord Northcliffe, as he was by then) boosted a play called *An Englishman's Home*, written by Captain du Maurier, a son of the Du Maurier of 'Trilby' fame. In *An Englishman's Home* the enemy was called 'The Empress of the North', but at that time everybody knew that this was but a synonym for Germany. In 1897, however, France was the feared enemy. We had had the Fashoda incident. What days for the new reading public! There came into the public eye a certain Colonel Kitchener, a handsome soldier who went to Khartoum to avenge Gordon. There went with him a *Daily Mail* correspondent named G. W. Steevens, who wrote for the boys of those days a book which outvied G. A. Henty: *With Kitchener to Khartoum*, and *The Charge of the 21st Lancers at the Battle of Omdurman*. What a story! The *Daily Mail* had broken into the barbed-wire entanglements of the class papers. It was now being read, coyly enough at first, in middle-class homes.

Schoolboys read it; I was one of them. I came from a typical middle-class home, where we read the *Daily Telegraph*; I, surreptitiously, read the *Daily Mail*. It was exciting. We lived in the Harmsworth legend, the 'local boy who had made good'. Our parents held him up as a good example; it was the period when parents preached the gospel of 'getting on in the world'. I remember so vividly a battalion of one of the Guards regiments which used from time to time to march past our house, about breakfast-time. One day my step-father, watching the marching men, said to me: 'Now, if you joined *them*, and became an officer, I would have some respect for you', and for some fleeting moments I had visions of myself going to Trafalgar Square and letting myself be accosted by one of the recruiting sergeants, with ribbons in this caps, of taking the 'Queen's shilling' and 'going for a soldier', as people said. Such was the influence of the Harmsworth legend.

Alfred Harmsworth worked like ten men. Gone were the indolent days mentioned by Sir Max Pemberton. The *Daily Mail* circulation figures of the period are eloquent in themselves. In 1896, the average daily net sale was 202,077; two years later when the Boer War broke out, it was 610,323, and in 1900—989,255. In 1902, the figure had fallen to 807,638, and the figures, with the exception of the year 1904, the year Alfred Harmsworth was made a baronet, continued to fall, until 1914.

It has been said that the Boer War did good to the *Daily Mail*, but there is no evidence that this war, the last of Britain's Imperial wars, did any more good to the *Daily Mail* than other newspapers.

In the Boer War, Alfred Harmsworth's superb powers of news organisation found full vent. Here came to the fore as war correspondents, Charles Hands, an ex-private soldier named Edgar Wallace, and the already mentioned G. W. Steevens, who was in besieged Ladysmith and died of enteric.

It was during the Boer War, in 1900, that the leading string of the Harmsworth team ran into a spate of trouble, but it was not in South Africa, it was in far-away China that the disaster occurred. What was known as the 'Boxer Rebellion' broke out, when foreign missionaries were attacked. A number of British subjects took refuge in the British Legation in Pekin. The *Daily Mail* published a full story of their massacre, and a memorial service was being arranged in Westminster Abbey, when the news was received that the *Daily Mail* story—published, of course, in all good faith—was false. It must have been a deadly body-blow to Alfred Harmsworth. Around the West End of London a mocking sheet was offered for sale, entitled the *Daily Liar*. The result of the *gaffe* was shown in the figures of the average daily net sale for the next year, which exhibited a loss of approximately 150,000, and the following year there was another drop of 30,000, and the year after a drop of more than

35,000: a loss in daily circulation of more than 215,000
in three years!

It is probable, however, that this sensational loss of
circulation during the period under review was, in
1903 at all events, not entirely due to the episode in
China.

In 1903 Alfred Harmsworth showed a serious absence
of political *flair*, during the Joseph Chamberlain
Tariff Reform Campaign.

The newly-founded *Daily Express*, launched by
Arthur Pearson, supported Chamberlain one hundred
per cent. What attitude was Alfred Harmsworth going
to take towards his hero? He wobbled, most indubitably, he wobbled.

In the earliest years of the *Daily Mail*, Harmsworth
himself edited the paper; in his absence Kennedy
Jones functioned, but soon Mr Thomas Marlowe was
appointed and remained in the editorial chair during
the best years of the *Daily Mail*. Alfred Harmsworth
was, however, the driving force. He knew many things,
but he did not know what attitude to take when
Chamberlain split Britain in two. In the beginning,
Harmsworth tried to convert the Liberal Lord Rosebery, his neighbour in Berkeley Square, to Tariff
Reform. Sir Almeric Fitzroy, who was very much
behind the scenes in those days, wrote: 'Rosebery
quarrelled with Northcliffe over Tariff Reform, when
Northcliffe tried to influence Rosebery. Northcliffe
hated financial losses.'

According to Sir Max Pemberton, Northcliffe's
powers were at their zenith in 1904, when Edward VII
was King and when on the advice of A. J. Balfour he
made Alfred Harmsworth a baronet; two years later
he was made a peer.

Edward VII had the greatest respect for the acumen

of the two Harmsworth brothers, Alfred and Harold, and often when there were knotty problems to be solved, the cry: 'Send for the Harmsworths!' was heard in Buckingham Palace.

If Pemberton's statement concerning the zenith of Northcliffe's powers is correct, it nevertheless conflicts more than somewhat with the statements of those who were in daily contact with the Chief. They are almost unanimous in calling attention to his growing arrogance, his daily fits of petulance and irritability. As regards his grip on the *Daily Mail*, I have already recorded the opinion of one of Pemberton's friends, a member of the *Daily Mail* staff, who, in 1903, remarked that the Chief had begun to relax personal grip on the details of the paper. Even Pemberton writes: 'Naturally Lord Northcliffe had peevish and petulant moments . . .' and he also quotes this most significant Northcliffian remark: 'I don't wonder that proprietors (of newspapers) end up in madhouses.'

Unreasonableness may perhaps be found about this time, when Northcliffe refused to permit pipe-smoking in the *Daily Mail* offices!

To what source can one trace these petty fits of ill-humour? Was it over-strain? Certainly Northcliffe was working hard; at six in the morning he was already on the job, but, on the credit side, according to what he himself told his intimates, he retired to bed at nine-thirty and by ten o'clock he was fast asleep. He took up golf in early middle age and became—by what he termed concentration—a good player, but even with this relaxation he could not entirely divorce himself from his newspaper affairs. Mr Tom Clarke relates: 'On Saturday, June 3 (1922), a message came to me from his (the Chief's) secretary. This was the day of the qualifying round at Bramshot for the

Northcliffe Gold Cup, and apparently he looked on it as a test of my progress in golf. He had been sending Sandy Thompson (Northcliffe's private "pro") every Friday to drill me, so that, he said, I should surprise the golf experts in the office. He had insisted on keeping these golf lessons a secret, "for I want you to give Sir Andrew Caird (the Head of the Financial Department of the *Daily Mail*) a shock by beating him!" The message from the Chief's secretary was that the Chief had instructed him to say I should be sacked if I failed to qualify. Luckily I scraped through.' At that time Mr Tom Clarke was News Editor of the *Daily Mail*.

Despite the hard work Northcliffe put into the *Daily Mail*, the average net sales of the newspaper continued to decline. At one time he tried to start a Sunday edition, and this attempt was copied by some rival publications, but they all had to cease publication owing to the opposition of the 'Nonconformist Conscience' which, apparently, did not understand that Sunday newspapers are made on Saturdays, whereas Monday morning newspapers, to which, seemingly, the 'Conscience' does not object, are made on the Lord's Day.

However, Northcliffe purchased the Sunday newspaper, *Weekly Dispatch*, and made a success of that.

Why did the *Daily Mail* figures droop from 1904 until 1914? Was it due to the opposition newspaper, the *Daily Express*, the poorly-financed halfpenny newspaper started by Sir Arthur Pearson? Pearson and Northcliffe had much in common, although Pearson was a better educated man in the ordinary acceptance of the phrase. Both were 'hustlers', both were men of quick temper, but there was no arrogance or megalomania in Pearson's mentality. He was a kind and gentle person who quite often, if he 'sacked' a man in a fit of temper, would rescind the sentence in a calmer moment and increase the man's salary. But it was Pearson's fate, largely due to inadequate finance, to always lag behind his competitor, a competition which culminated in the struggle for possession of *The Times*, a story which is related in its proper place. This, however, must be said. Harmsworth was the pioneer, the master-mind behind the first attempt in Great Britain to control mass thought, although, as a personal opinion, I much doubt whether Northcliffe in the first years in the life of the *Daily Mail* had any intention of exercising such control; like Topsy, it 'just growed', but if there had been no *Daily Mail*, there would have been no *Daily Express*.

The moment has come to discuss the ingredients which made up the success of the *Daily Mail*, not merely its success as a money-maker, but of its pioneering influence on British life at a moment when the history of Britain was at a turning point. How much was due to the personal influence of Northcliffe inside and outside of the *Daily Mail*, and how much is traceable to his power to capitalise the favours of the Goddess Luck? Was the success entirely the outcome of the financial genius of his brother Harold, the first Lord Rothermere? What part, great or small, may be attributed to those who wrote the *Daily Mail*?

In the next chapter you will find my attempt to deal with the parts played by those who wrote and managed the *Daily Mail* during Northcliffe's lifetime.

Northcliffe has often been called a 'great journalist'. Was he? And in any case, what exactly is a journalist? To try to answer the second question, firstly I would say that fundamentally a journalist is a person who writes a journal, a maker of notes, a person who

reports, hence a reporter. But the person who prepares
the report for the newspaper, the sub-editor, is also
entitled to call himself a journalist. His responsibilities
are greater than those of the reporter, but although
he may legitimately call himself a journalist, the sub-
editor plays no part in the obtaining of reports, the
news, the gathering of the facts on which each and
every newspaper lives. The news editor is the man who
provides the assignments for the reporters, who
dispatches them on their fact-finding quests. The news
editor is a man who has graduated from the ranks of
the reporters. Yet, good as a news editor may be, if he
has behind or above him a man who is what the French
call an *animateur*, a man who may be what in modern
parlance is known as an idea merchant, that news
editor is going to be a better equipped news editor, a
happy combination which will be of indirect assistance
to the reporters, hence to the newspaper itself. Northcliffe was the first newspaper proprietor in Britain to
supply that useful driving force to his newspaper. He
knew.

As an illuminating instance of what I have in my
mind, I can do no better than quote a statement made
to me by one of Northcliffe's former secretaries. When
Northcliffe was living at Sutton Place, Surrey, he
drove one day to London accompanied by this secretary. The car was on a road alongside the Thames at
a place where some barges were moored. Suddenly
Northcliffe ordered the car to stop. 'Those women
[the bargees' wives] are wearing the same hats you
see in the Leach drawings', he said to his secretary.
'Go and ask them where they get them.' The secretary
obtained the information. Northcliffe ordered a story
to be obtained and published. A small thing, possibly,
but the world we live in is made up of small things,

and some of them, many of them, are interesting
things: the things which were in *Tit-Bits*, the journalistic god-father of the *Daily Mail* and its imitators.
The story of the bargees' wives may be called journalism, but Northcliffe's functions in the *Daily Mail* were
not confined to the obtaining of tit-bits of information.
Wickham Steed related in his book, *The Press*, how the
Chief himself edited the paper in the early days. He
realised that the new Public for which he was catering
could not concentrate on long articles. He decided
that nothing, except in very special circumstances,
should exceed three hundred words, and these three
hundred words were cut down into short paragraphs,
in order to be easy on the eye. There you have the
functions of the sub-editor, not the reporter. Yet a
good reporter must be something more than a gatherer
of facts; he must know how to marshal his facts, and,
still more, he must write them vividly. Did Northcliffe
write vividly? My suggestion is that he did not. His
writings all his life bore the stamp of the school
magazine, something like his early efforts: 'Some
Curious Types of Butterflies'. Neither was he a particularly good judge of writing. He read very little himself;
he was not 'keen on reading', as he himself said. One
must look elsewhere for other ingredients in the success
of the *Daily Mail*.

An episode which illustrates another angle of
Northcliffe's exceptional clear-sightedness in the
journalistic field, was when he heard of a book that
was not selling. He gave orders for an article about
'the book that will not sell'. Both the publisher and
the author were furious; why make bad worse? The
book was about the German Peril. The gist of the
article was that here was a good, well-written book,
but nobody would read it. Why? Send your ideas on a
E

post-card to the Editor and you have a chance to win
£100. You see the idea? Back to the days of *Answers*,
which meant, back to *Tit-Bits* again. Naturally, the
boost sold the book, so the author and the publisher
were content, but you must understand that Northcliffe merely used the book as what he called a
'talking point' to make people talk about the *Daily
Mail*. He was always seeking and finding 'talking
points'. Make people talk about something they will
read in the *Daily Mail*. Out of this motto of his, Northcliffe built up the 'stunt'. You may say, well, if his
'stunts' were so clever, how was it that the *Daily Mail*
circulation continued to fall? I think the answer is
this: if there had been no 'stunts', the loss in circulation
would well have been greater.

     The best-known *Daily Mail* stunts were the Standard
Bread and the Sweet Pea stunts. 'Talking points' these
were so obviously, but the famous Kipling poem, 'The
Absent-Minded Beggar', published in the *Daily Mail*
and which raised £100,000 for a South African War
charity, was likewise just a 'stunt'. One must wonder
in retrospection how many—or how few—of the
readers of the *Daily Mail* realised this at the time.
Northcliffe brought from the U.S. the already
mentioned 'stunt merchant', Mr Charles Balch, to
run the Kipling stunt.

     These things, trivial as they may be, did not justify,
however, Lord Salisbury's gibe at the *Daily Mail*: 'a
newspaper produced by office boys for office boys'.
Anyhow, Salisbury was but paraphrasing from
Thackeray's 'Pendennis', when there was question of
starting a new paper which was to be produced 'by
gentlemen for gentlemen'.

     After his famous 'wobble' on Chamberlain's Tariff
Reform, when he finally came out for Protection and

saw Protection defeated, Northcliffe decided there were to be no more political stunts in the *Daily Mail*, but he changed his mind during the first World War.

The '*Daily Mail* Hat' was another stunt, but one produced when Northcliffe's mental powers had seriously deteriorated. People did talk, but they also laughed, not with it but at the *Daily Mail*. One unrecorded by-product of this occurred in Paris where Northcliffe was staying while this stunt was in operation. A former member of the *Daily Mail*, the late Henry Noble Hall, who had been sacked, procured with great trouble a model of the '*Daily Mail* Hat' and wore it. He walked up and down the corridor of the Ritz Hotel outside the Northcliffe suite, hoping to be noticed and reinstated, but, as the actor Rutland Barrington used to say of theatrical 'flops', 'it failed to attract'.

In 1910, Northcliffe again played the same stunt he had used during his abortive attempt to win Portsmouth in the Unionist interest and in his publication *Answers*—the invasion stunt. This was now reproduced in the *Daily Mail* in the form of a serial by the late William Le Queux. The main feature of the story, which had chapters secretly written by Lord Roberts and a member of the *Daily Mail* staff named H. W. Wilson, was 'The Siege of London'.

Lord Roberts, the famous 'Bobs', and Mr Wilson together drafted the probable route which an invading Germany army landing in England would take; their ideas had to be subjected to the approval of Lord Northcliffe. When he was shown the German line of march, according to Lord Roberts and Mr Wilson, Northcliffe caustically remarked that from a military point of view it might be all right, but from a circulation point of view it was all wrong. No matter what

Lord Roberts thought, Germans must pass through sizeable towns, and not through small villages where there was little possibility of large *Daily Mail* sales. To appease Northcliffe, the German invaders' road became a little zig-zag. Nothing like what a German general would plan, but according to an intimate of North-cliffe, the story still appealed to the credulity of readers.

Northcliffe never had any illusions about his readers.

This point has direct connection with other points made by Northcliffe's intimates; one calls his former Chief a bluffer; he relates how, having learned a fact, he would pretend to have always known it and would discuss the matter at meals, so as to snub those whom he found honest enough to express ignorance of the matter under discussion. This characteristic trait, however, may be bracketed with his schoolboyish love of making a mystery out of little or nothing. It was harmless enough and sometimes amusing. A more serious side to the bluffing and the playing on the credulity of the public may be found in something Sir Max Pemberton has to say.

Pemberton, when he had known Northcliffe for twenty-two years, heard from the lips of the Chief an alleged happening in a Spanish cathedral, a sup-posedly eye-witness account of how a living woman had been walled up in a pillar of the cathedral. Pemberton wrote this story, which was duly published. The Catholic Truth Society attacked Pemberton, who took the matter up with the Chief. Northcliffe laughed and said he had 'made up' the story. This was quite untrue, because the story in question is one of the lies most often related by professing anti-Roman Catholics. There seems little doubt, unfortunately, that North-cliffe fell for the story, and passed it on to a man who had worked for his publications over a period of years.

Under Northcliffe's direction, Culture became a 'stunt', as also did the Russo-Japanese War. When I was a boy, the Harmsworth Encyclopedia appeared—in fortnightly parts: Culture at cut rates. Judged in retrospect, it was not a good encyclopedia, but no doubt it served its purpose—to the publishers, at least.

The Russo-Japanese War caused Harmsworth to issue a weekly publication: *Japan's Fight for Freedom*—a much-biased title and entirely misleading, for both Russia and Japan fought an Imperialistic war. It was yet another instance of the credulity of the readers.

People know about such Northcliffian stunts as Standard Bread (which Northcliffe said was the cheapest stunt he ever worked) and Sweet Peas; some people may remember the Soap stunt which involved Northcliffe in a libel suit which cost the *Daily Mail* a quarter of a million sterling, but perhaps the least-known was the Prince of Wales stunt. In my opinion it was certainly the best, because the public never realised it was just a 'stunt' and, in any case, it 'put over' the Prince of Wales and made him exactly what the *Daily Mail* called him: 'Our Young Man'.

Many readers, no doubt, will recall that smiling photograph of the young Prince in naval uniform; that began the 'build-up' which continued until 'Our Young Man' was not only the hero of Great Britain but of the United States as well. It is on record that during his first visit to New York, the late Mr Ochs showed the young Prince over the premises of the great newspaper he owned, the *New York Times*. During the visit, Mr Ochs remarked with a smile: 'D'you know, Sir, you are so popular over here, we could elect you President of these United States?'

To which the Prince of Wales is said to have replied: 'Don't you think, Mr Ochs, that I have a pretty important post awaiting me?' He had, and the British Press, pioneered by Northcliffe's *Daily Mail*, made the British public Prince-of-Wales conscious. There may have been other stunts which achieved as much lasting good as the 'Our Young Man' stunt, but I do not know of them.

Northcliffe's attitude towards stunts may be summed up as: 'anything that will make people talk'. Anything that would convince advertisers of their pulling power of his papers was material for a stunt. Northcliffe had a genius for finding such material and worked on it with great enthusiasm. Once he made a stunt of saving the Crystal Palace. Someone said to him: 'Why do you want to save that awful place? It ought to be blown up!' He answered with a mischievous grin: 'I'd just as soon raise a subscription to blow it up'.

What did Northcliffe actually accomplish during his twenty-six years association with the *Daily Mail*? Mr Tom Clarke records a list of such things as getting telephones put into police stations, a list that reads as if it might have been culled from a parish magazine. What Northcliffe accomplished inside the *Daily Mail* was actually far more than any parochial list of mundane things. Were I required to put the matter into one sentence, I would say that he dramatised the humdrum things of life, made life itself more exciting at a time when people's brains were sluggish; but he did not do this entirely 'off his own bat'. Hamilton Fyfe wrote that 'Without K.J.'s professional knowledge, his skill in picking useful men, his ruthless discard of those who are not useful, the *Daily Mail* could not have won its immediate and permanent success'.

What does all this add up to? Perhaps, maybe, Kennedy Jones' favourite remark had a permanent sting. He used to say: 'Nothing really matters'.

NEWSPAPER campaigns are mostly empirical and whether they bring credit or glory to their progenitors is a matter that had better be left over for discussion, but in most of the campaigns of which Northcliffe was the prime mover, values were of less importance to him than the vital necessity of making people talk about a subject he chose for them. Many of what he called 'talking points' interested him personally not at all, but his vision as a newspaper proprietor was clear and in most instances his judgment of his own ability to make his readers 'talk' was completely sound. Take aviation. It is, of course, a fact that the public reaction to a certain kind of bread was the same as its reaction to aviation, that is to say it was wholly favourable, but Northcliffe was able to provide both bread and circuses for his readers. One of the best circuses he ever produced was the aerial circus. For a time he made a corner in aerial affairs. If this brought him no other reward, it did bring him, in the closing years of his life, an offer from Mr Lloyd George to become Air Minister, a post Northcliffe refused.

Northcliffe's vision concerning aviators was as clear as his vision concerning aviation; he predicted that the French would play a leading part in the develop-

ment of the science of aviation and the early history
of aviation proves the forecast to have been completely
correct.

When the Wright brothers began their experiments
at Pau, Northcliffe was among those who watched
them, but he watched them with amused tolerance;
he said he thought their methods too clumsy. As usual,
he was interested in the ends and not in the means. If a
man was going to fly, why then, let him fly. He did
not use his influence to help the Wrights with either
encouragement or applause.

In 1896, the year Northcliffe launched the *Daily
Mail*, a wealthy young Brazilian named Santos-
Dumont made a short flight near Paris in a heavier-
than-air machine. One of Northcliffe's biographers
affirms that Northcliffe witnessed the flight, but I
understand he knew nothing of the flight until he saw
a brief account of it in the *Daily Mail* and telephoned
to Carmelite House complaining that the report had
been inadequately displayed.

Santos-Dumont was no novice in the air; some seven
years before the *Daily Mail* was launched, the young
Brazilian was experimenting with a one-man controlled (Santos-Dumont was the man) gas-filled
envelope, carrying a small motor. The Brazilian's aim
was to fly round the Eiffel Tower. He had hair-
breadth escapes from death, and subsequently turned
his attention, with small success, to heavier-than-air
machines.

Northcliffe saw the possibility of creating a sensational 'talking point'; he offered a prize of £1,000 to
the man who first flew the English Channel. This offer
created considerable talk, but none came forward to
make the attempt. In France there was much more
interest in flying than there was in Britain, but never-

theless, not even a Frenchman was prepared to try and win the *Daily Mail* prize. Northcliffe was very angry and as usual he looked around for someone on whom he could lay the blame. His Paris office was the object of his attack. A member of the Paris staff, named Macabe, was instructed to find someone willing to make the attempt. Macabe went to a flying meeting at Rheims, where he met a former motor mechanic named Bleriot, who had interested himself in aviation and who had made an airplane. Macabe induced Bleriot to enter for the prize and promised that all his expenses would be paid. In 1909, Bleriot was ready, but the well-boosted news of Bleriot's entry brought forward another entry, that of a rich young Frenchman of British origin, named Hubert Latham. Both men set up their camps at Sangatte, near Calais. Now that there were two Richmonds in the field, the whole of Britain was excitedly interested in this attempt to fly the Channel; the sporting spirit being evoked and a corps of bright reporters posted on both sides of the Channel, the stage was set for a brilliant North-cliffian stunt.

At this time the front page of the *Daily Mail* was devoted to advertisements only; the chief proprietor steadfastly refused to emulate its younger rival, the *Daily Express*, and put news on the front page; it was curious how at a moment when Northcliffe was banging the big drum for all he was worth and boosting progress, and calling attention to men flying like birds, he should cling to old-fashioned methods of presenting news; but despite this, the *Daily Mail* was lengths ahead of all its rivals.

After many false alarms and disappointments, Bleriot flew the Channel and won the £1,000 prize.

Having used the offered reward as a 'talking point'

for readers—and, of course, as a justified method of seeking new readers—Northcliffe now turned his attention to his clients in the advertising world.

The machine in which Bleriot had flown the Channel was placed on show at Selfridge's, in Oxford Street, London. Northcliffe gave a banquet at which Bleriot was the guest of honour. The majority of his guests were those who spent the most money in his advertisement columns.

But Northcliffe was only just beginning his own conquest of the air. He rented a furnished house in Rheims, where most of the important French aviation meetings were held, and made a point of inviting airmen to the house and entertaining them lavishly. Within a year of the successful Channel flight he promoted a £10,000 prize for the first flight from London to Manchester. Another Frenchman, Paulhan, won this.

Two years later, Northcliffe promoted a Round-Britain Air Race which was won by yet another Frenchman who captured the £10,000 prize. The next prize, for a trans-Atlantic flight, was won by two Britishers, Messrs Alcock and Brown.

It is easy enough to attribute unworthy motives to a man who uses a scientific invention to boost his business, which is just what Northcliffe did, but his motives were just, according to his own lights, and certainly not unworthy; but were they as altruistic as his sycophants would have us believe?

If one is very rich and the chief proprietor of many publications, there are many things one can do; if, additionally, one has the genius for purveying news and views, there is practically no limit to the scope one has of making people read and talk about the things one thinks they should read and talk about.

That is what is called the Power of the Press. Many people exaggerate the Power of the Press. The Press, I would suggest, cannot enforce action. It can make people talk and, to a limited extent, make them think. The British Press has, occasionally, raised public outcry sufficiently loudly for Authority to take notice, but in the main the result of the reaction of the public to the outcry raised is in disproportion to the noise. Sometimes it may happen that a man or woman wrongfully treated by justice has had his or her case revised as a result of newspaper clamour, and undoubtedly such cases must be chalked up on the credit side of British newspaperdom. Sometimes it may happen that a newspaper will clamour for a fund to be raised and reward made. Some such funds had real merit and just reward is their target. Sometimes, as in the case of a fund raised more than a half-century ago by the *Daily Telegraph* for the cricketer, Dr W. G. Grace, the fund becomes somewhat of a newspaper stunt. Indeed, it is extremely difficult to draw a straight line dividing the altruistic and the not-so-altruistic aims of any newspaper which clamours for this or that to be done. Some members of the newspaper-reading public are always so ready to suggest unworthy motives for a newspaper campaign; they insist that Lord Blank must have shares in this or that concern which they imagine is going to benefit financially by this or that booming or boosting. This is not straight thinking, although it may superficially seem logical and human. In the first place a person with such thoughts should pause for a moment to consider and reflect; he might then understand that no British newspaper proprietor would use such crude methods to increase his wealth. Secondly, he should understand that operating any organ of what is called

the popular or national Press is just a business, like
selling steel or chemicals or margarine. The aim of the
business is to keep up or increase profits, and this can
be done only by keeping up or increasing advertising
revenue. To keep up or increase advertising revenue,
the newspaper proprietor must keep up or increase his
number of readers. To keep up or increase his number
of readers, he must keep his public interested, keep it
talking, giving it tit-bits of news, advice, views and,
occasionally, a body-jolting surprise.

One wet morning in Cannes, I asked Lord Beaverbrook how he had made a success of the *Daily Express*,
which, incidentally, he had purchased when it was a
most excellently written and edited newspaper, but in
financially low water. Without a second's hesitation,
Lord Beaverbrook replied: 'I increased its market'.
What a sentence of wisdom! I strongly recommend it
to all would-be newspaper proprietors. All you have
to do is to purchase a newspaper and increase its
market. That can most certainly be done nowadays if
you have the money and the financial genius to
increase the market. Fortunately, Lord Beaverbrook
had both. But Lord Beaverbrook also had good fortune
on his side, the good fortune being that Lord Northcliffe had already pioneered the path.

For a number of years Northcliffe made the air a
subject particularly his own—that is to say, he made
it a prominent 'talking point' of the *Daily Mail*. It
might well be too much to claim that he made the
British public air-conscious, but there is enough
evidence to proclaim that he hastened the process by
directing mass thought towards aviation.

Lord Northcliffe never flew. To us this may sound
curious, but Northcliffe's absence from the air can be
regarded in better perspective if one remembers that

he died long before flying became so commonplace as it is today, when it was something of an adventure. Even some years after Northcliffe's death, when I discussed flying with another newspaper peer who was encouraging his staff to fly, I found he himself had never flown.

THERE are several versions, romantic, prosaic, or mysterious, of the manner in which Lord North-cliffe managed to acquire control of *The Times*. Undoubtedly he enjoyed wearing this cloak of mystery until he did eventually obtain control, but persons who should know the circumstances are in contra-diction one with the other, and all are in seeming contradiction with the official story as published (1947) in the third volume of the *History of The Times*.

The late Mr Wickham Steed, Foreign Editor and later Editor of *The Times*, gave me permission to publish his version of how Lord Northcliffe first heard that *The Times* was for sale.

Mr Steed said that the news which enabled North-cliffe to buy a controlling interest in *The Times* came to him because of his love of music and youthful skill as a pianist which enabled him to appreciate the genius of Paderewski. Northcliffe was invited to a party at the Stuart-Wortleys, where Paderewski was to play. But the night was so foggy that Northcliffe telephoned to say he could not go. His host urged him to make a special effort to come, saying that Paderewski would be playing some of Northcliffe's favourite music. So Northcliffe groped his way through the fog to the Stuart-Wortleys' house, where he met an acquaintance

who had just helped to amalgamate the more or less
bankrupt Great Central Railway with what was then
the Midland Railway. Northcliffe congratulated him
upon his achievement and was told in reply that
something more sensational was being done—the
amalgamation of the bankrupt *Standard* with *The Times*
under the management of Mr C. Arthur Pearson.

However, I cannot help wondering whether, even
in 1908, Paderewski played in private houses, and as
for playing Northcliffe's favourite music, no record
shows that Northcliffe was musical in the Paderewski
sense of the word. It is a fact that Northcliffe could
play by ear, but he never made any pretence of being
musical.

Sir Max Pemberton's version of the purchase of
The Times is slightly different. Sir Max records that
Lord Northcliffe remembered that Lord Fadingdon
was not only Chairman of the Great Central Railway,
but was also financially interested in the *Standard*
(also at one time in the *Daily Express*). Lord Northcliffe
also remembered that Sir George Lewis, the first Sir
George, the famous Society lawyer, was a friend of Mr
Moberly Bell, the manager of *The Times*. Northcliffe,
according to Sir Max, obtained confirmation that *The
Times* was going to be amalgamated from W. T. Stead,
with whom he quarrelled some years later. When
Stead informed him, Northcliffe caused a paragraph
to be inserted in *The Observer*, which he owned,
announcing a change in the ownership and management of *The Times*. This version, less romantic than
Mr Steed's version, nevertheless misses the one vital
point; it was a shareholder in *The Times* who made the
first approach to Lord Northcliffe; she wanted to sell
her share, a fortieth interest, to someone who knew
the newspaper business.

The shareholder was a Mrs Sibley, a grand-daughter of the first John Walter. Early in 1898, Dr Sibley, at his mother's behest, wrote a letter to Alfred Harmsworth, whom he did not know at all. A meeting was arranged when Harmsworth said he would buy the whole or any part of Mrs Sibley's interest in *The Times*. Alfred Harmsworth called at *The Times* offices in Printing House Square, only to be rebuffed; he was told he would not be allowed to purchase any part of Mrs Sibley's share.

Now Mr R. D. Blumenfeld comes into the narrative. I have already explained that Mr Blumenfeld, born in the United States, but who became a naturalised Englishman, was at one time News Editor of the *Daily Mail*, and later Editor of the *Daily Express*. Mr Blumenfeld had a varied and colourful life. He was sent to West Point by his father, as he was intended for the Army, but he had other ideas and at the age of twenty-one he was already the editor of a New York evening newspaper. James Gordon Bennett brought him to London as correspondent for the *New York Herald*. Later he and Mr Bennett parted company. Once when I was staying with Mr Blumenfeld at his Essex home, he told me that when he left Mr Bennett's employ he secretly thought he would never get a newspaper job again; so he obtained employment in London with the Hoe Printing Press. In the course of his business Mr Blumenfeld talked to Mr Godfrey Walter of *The Times* about the sale of printing machinery to *The Times*. This came to the knowledge of Alfred Harmsworth, who was then thirty-five years old. He wrote to Blumenfeld, asking him to make an offer on his behalf; Harmsworth said he had a million pounds locked up in Consols and authorised Blumenfeld to make an offer up to that amount.

Daily Mail

MILLION SALE.

3 P.M. TO-DAY

SATURDAY, JUNE 28, 1919

Daily Mail

MILLION SALE.

WHAT THE HUNS MUST DO NOW

MONDAY, JUNE 30, 1919

Times

AUGUST 5, 1914   1 D.

BRITAIN AT WAR

DON'T WAIT UNTIL YOUR HOME IS WRECKED REGISTER IN **Daily Mail** ZEPPELIN FUND TO-DAY

Imperial War Museum

Contents bills typical of Lord Northcliffe's famous 'talking points'.
1914-1919

Mr Blumenfeld wrote to Mr Godfrey Walter under date October, 1900, making the offer on Harmsworth's behalf. Mr Walter held up his reply for two months and then wrote declining discussion.

Nothing happened for two years, then Alfred Harmsworth wrote in May, 1902, to Mr Arthur Walter asking for a few minutes private conversation. He wished to discuss a Dr Sibley who had been making himself such a nuisance that he would have nothing to do with him.

The meeting took place; Harmsworth offered to buy a controlling interest in *The Times*. Mr Arthur Walter politely showed him the door.

There followed then a period of litigation in which Alfred Harmsworth had no part; it was confined solely to *The Times* shareholders, but it is certain that Harmsworth followed the litigation carefully, because it proved him to be right in his contention that *The Times* as an independent organ could no longer be regarded as a paying proposition.

Mr Moberly Bell, formerly the Egyptian correspondent of *The Times*, and for ten years its manager in London, had reached the same conclusion, but he did not propose to have *The Times* sold to Harmsworth or anybody else, although eventually he did. Moberly Bell now began making an attempt to save *The Times* by appending the name of the newspaper to publishing ventures. News of these ventures reached the United States, and more particularly the ears of two astute Americans, Horace Everett Hooper and William Montgomery Jackson. These two men had specialised in the United States in high-pressure book-selling, first of all buying up old plates, reprinting and then by-passing the bookshops, and selling books direct to the public.

F

Messrs Hooper and Jackson went to London and put a proposition to the manager of *The Times* and through him to the chief proprietor, Mr Walter. They offered to reprint the encyclopedia and sell it to the public on the instalment plan, but they wanted to call the reprint '*The Times* Edition'. Eventually they obtained permission. At this time, 1898, telegrams in Great Britain were associated with calamitous news; the sight of an orange-coloured envelope brought on attacks of near heart failure. The two Americans invoked the aid of the British Post Office to sell Culture; people were fetched out of their beds to tear open the flimsy envelopes, expecting Heaven knows what, but only to find an offer to sell them a set of the *Encyclopedia Britannica* at cut rate prices. Thousands protested, but hundreds purchased. The scheme was a great success, and *The Times* was happy; Messrs Hooper and Jackson had guaranteed a hundred columns of advertising and, moreover, were paying *The Times* a guinea royalty for every set sold.

The two Americans then persuaded *The Times* to allow them to start *The Times* Book Club. When Alfred Harmsworth heard of this, he predicted failure and for a while his prediction was correct; in fact it did not, as it was hoped, increase *The Times* circulation. But the influence of the two Americans within *The Times* increased, and there is little doubt that their drive and fund of ideas kept the great newspaper alive, but it was quite evident that, nevertheless, the newspaper was almost at the end of its resources. Sir Edgar Speyer, a banker of German origin, was known to be anxious to acquire *The Times*, and at this moment Messrs Hooper and Jackson put forward their own offer to buy the paper. Both the Americans had met 'young Harmsworth' and had been impressed by his alertness and activity, but whether he was to stand in with the deal—if it came off—has never transpired. After prolonged negotiations and discussions, Mr Walter decided not to accept the American offer.

Mr Walter now decided to form a company to control *The Times* to bring in fresh capital and to run the newspaper in a more modern and efficient manner. The advice of Lord Rothschild and Lord Lansdowne was sought and obtained; in the course of talks the name of Sir Alexander Henderson was introduced; he was a respected City man and had financial interests in the *Daily Express* and *Standard*. Sir Alexander was asked to find a person with technical knowledge to advise on the reconstruction of the paper; it was perfectly natural that he should suggest the editor of one of the newspapers in which he was financially interested: Mr Arthur Pearson. The only thing was that Pearson was Harmsworth's rival, and Harmsworth, when he heard of the move, was furiously angry. He must have become more angry when he discovered that Pearson had done much more than to act in an advisory capacity; he proposed to join the board of the new company, with his brother-in-law, and to amalgamate the *Standard* with *The Times*. These negotiations were kept secret from the editorial staff of *The Times* and from the shareholders, and, most important, from Moberly Bell. They obtained the first news from a paragraph in *The Observer*, which belonged to the Harmsworth Group. On Sunday, January 5, 1908, *The Observer* said: 'It is understood that important negotiations are taking place which will place the direction of *The Times* newspaper in the hands of a very capable proprietor of several popular magazines and newspapers.' The general view was that the 'capable proprietor' was Alfred Harmsworth

himself, and, maybe, that is what Northcliffe wished
people to think. In any case, Mr Godfrey Walter
thought so, and he gave instructions that *The Times*
should immediately publish a paragraph naming
Mr C. Arthur Pearson as 'the proposed managing
director'. When Bell saw a draft of the paragraph, he
wrote a note to the chief proprietor, with whom he
had been on terms of close friendship for twenty years,
saying how hurt he was at the lack of confidence shown
in him. Apart from this, Bell, who had an ear closer to
the ground of Fleet Street than the chief proprietor,
knew that quite recently there had been rumours
concerning the financial stability of the *Standard*.
Nevertheless, the plan went forward, although the
reception of *The Times* paragraph was not wholly
favourable.

Moberly Bell was openly opposed to the Pearson
project; at this time he had turned sixty, but was full
of fight and a desire to form a company of his own to
control *The Times* and he might have succeeded had it
not been for Northcliffe.

For some years Northcliffe had made it a practice
to go abroad when he was planning some sensational
coup. For two months he had been closely watching
The Times. Now he was at the Ritz Hotel in Paris, but
his close watch did not prevent him exhibiting the
interest he invariably took in something that momen-
tarily seized his attention. Now it was hotels, the
management and the running of them. Madame Ritz
relates that Northcliffe plied the reception clerks with
questions and took an opportunity of going behind
the reception desk and delightedly booking in an
American family.

It was while he was in Paris that *The Observer* paragraph was concocted.

As soon as Pearson signed the draft agreement with *The Times* he talked about it very freely. The news of it came by a roundabout route to the always attentive ears of Sir George Lewis, the already mentioned London lawyer; he passed it on to Mr George Sutton, manager of the *Daily Mail* and a client of Sir George Lewis. Sutton telegraphed the information to Northcliffe, who replied telling Sutton to come to Paris at once for a conference. As a result of the conference the paragraph was drafted and telegraphed by Sutton to *The Observer*.

On the day after publication, news editors sent reporters to interview Northcliffe, Pearson and Newnes; they could not locate Northcliffe, who, of course, was in Paris; Newnes said the paragraph could not possibly refer to him because he was not interested in *The Times*. But Pearson allowed himself to be interviewed. He would not give a denial, but said there was nothing in it—for the moment, thus practically confirming that it was he to whom the paragraph referred. In other words he walked, eyes wide open, into the Northcliffe trap.

The news was published that Pearson was going to purchase *The Times*.

In Carmelite House, Sutton, and Kennedy Jones, at Northcliffe's behest, 'kept the pot boiling', blowing on the glowing embers of rumours to keep them alive. Cables passed to and fro between Carmelite House and the Ritz, Paris, but the cables were not addressed *en clair* to Northcliffe; they were addressed to his Austrian valet, Brunnbauer. The *Daily Mail* was building up a story to try to kill the ultimate control of *The Times* by Arthur Pearson.

It was rare drama, full of mystery such as Northcliffe loved.

The plot thickened; the two astute Americans, Hooper and Jackson, were in it and Bell was with them. The main idea was to create an impression among the public that the Walter family was willing to make secure the printing business by sacrificing the dignity of *The Times*. The word 'hustle' had crossed the Atlantic and had entered the English language. Arthur Pearson was known as a hustler, but the verb 'to hustle' was the last one one could imagine being conjugated in Printing House Square. As *The Times* states in its final summing up of instructions for Foreign Correspondents, '*The Times* prefers to report news in the past sense'. But the story the *Daily Mail* was preparing for publication did not follow *The Times* precept; the *Daily Mail* was preparing a coming event in order that it should cast a shadow.

Arthur Pearson was a fervent supporter of Mr Joseph Chamberlain and his Tariff Reform Programme. The *Daily Mail* story quoted Mr Chamberlain as saying: 'Mr Pearson is the greatest hustler I have ever known.' The story, as it appeared, seemed on the surface to heap praise and congratulations on Mr Pearson, but the general impression, the one Northcliffe wished to create, was: 'Heaven help *The Times* if Pearson gets control of it'.

Pearson was a charming person, but when he was roused, his temper could equal Northcliffe's. At this moment, however, he was full of guilelessness; he swallowed every word of the *Daily Mail* praise, really and truly believing it to be genuine.

In Paris an autobiographical sketch of Pearson was written for the *Daily Mail*; it was signed: 'By an Opponent', but the sketch, too, was charming, and disarming, indeed Northcliffe sent the proof to Pearson and addressed it to *The Times*, pretending to believe that the deal had already gone through! (He had written the story himself.) The accompanying letter said that Northcliffe had only just that moment heard of the 'deal'. Then came a telegram, also sent to *The Times*, and full of congratulations.

Pearson was completely taken in; he cabled back his thanks and said: 'Your generosity is overwhelming'. Pearson also wrote a letter saying how touched he was. The same day friends of Pearson's made him see the truth and how he had been the victim of a clever plot. Anxious to repair some at least of the harm he had done to his prospects of controlling *The Times*, Pearson gave out an authoritative statement saying: '*The Times* is to remain *The Times* in the best and fullest sense of the word.' But it was too late.

On Northcliffe's instructions, Kennedy Jones contacted the American Hooper and wrung from him an admission that he would like to see Pearson beaten. This important meeting—a vital move in the sale of *The Times*—concluded with Hooper advising 'K.J.' to see Bell and promising that he himself would arrange a *rendezvous*.

Hooper kept his word and advised Bell to try to help Northcliffe to buy *The Times*; Bell refused, but he did agree to meet Kennedy Jones. As a result of this meeting, another cable went to the Austrian valet; it was signed 'Kay Jay'. The cable told Northcliffe that the way was clear for him to go ahead and purchase *The Times*. But was the way clear?

Moberly Bell had been doing some thinking since his meeting with 'Kay Jay'; he reached the conclusion, possibly correctly, that his personality guaranteed the sobriety, austerity and dignity of *The Times*; for *The Times* to prevent revolutionary measures touching it, it would be necessary for a potential purchaser to

guarantee to retain the editorial staff of the newspaper
en bloc. Meanwhile in Paris a curious situation had
arisen.

The January gales had delayed postal and tele-
graphic communications between the British and
French capitals. Northcliffe, without news from his
agents in London, thought that possibly by now
Pearson *had* obtained virtual control of *The Times*.
Therefore, so his volatile mind concluded, he had
malgré lui done the right thing in sending Pearson his
congratulations. Northcliffe wrote Sutton a very long
and self-revealing letter.

He told Sutton that the reason why he did not want
Kennedy-Jones or anybody else to go to Paris was
because everything that went on in Carmelite House
was known, so he said. He then developed a plan to
obtain control of *The Times*, and have Pearson as
managing director. Northcliffe wrote that Pearson's
vanity would keep him at Printing House Square
fourteen hours a day; Pearson would neglect the
Daily Express and the *Standard*, and these properties
would be ruined, so Carmelite House would
benefit.

A renewal of the ever-recurring *Times* litigation by
shareholders was down for hearing; time was pressing.
Northcliffe went to London under an assumed name
and stayed with George Sutton. Bell wrote asking to
see him, plaintively saying: 'Couldn't I go out to some
suburb and you pick me up in a motor?' But Northcliffe did not meet him. He left London and went to
Boulogne. While he was there a story went about that
two Americans intended purchasing *The Times*.
Northcliffe returned to London and met Bell at an
office in Sackville Street, where he said to Bell: 'Well,
Mr Bell, I am going to buy *The Times* with your

assistance, if you will give it; without if you will not.'
Northcliffe charmed Bell by saying he did not intend
to make any changes whatsoever in the conduct of
The Times; perhaps it is not unfair to suggest that he
completed his charming of Moberly Bell when he
asked him how much *The Times* was paying him at
present and then offered him the post of managing
director in the new company.

Northcliffe insisted that his name should never be
divulged while the negotiations were in progress; he
was to be 'Mr X'. When Northcliffe returned to
Boulogne, Bell visited him disguised as 'Mr Moberly'.
When Bell returned to London, Northcliffe never
communicated directly with him; he wrote to Mrs
Bell, who transmitted the messages to her husband in
Arabic!

Northcliffe had 'news items' circulated saying that
he was in the South of France; in reality he was going
backwards and forwards between Versailles, Boulogne
and London; when in London he stayed incognito,
either with George Sutton in Belsize Park, near where
he used to live as a child, or else with one of his
secretaries in a block of flats near Victoria.

Northcliffe made up an elaborate code. He referred
to himself as 'Atlantic' based on 'Emperor of the
Atlantic', which the Kaiser had called himself when
he flagged a message to the Czar of Russia. Northcliffe
was very obsessed about a story that the Kaiser wanted
to buy *The Times*.

In the code, Printing House Square was referred to
as 'The Cenotaph'. Northcliffe's brother, Harold, who
drafted the financial clauses of the purchase, was
Abigail; Sutton was Buffalo, Kennedy Jones,
Alberta. Bell was at first Canton, but later, he
went again to Boulogne disguised as 'Mr Charles

Ball'. Of course all passports did not exist, so it was possible for grown-ups to play childish games of this nature.

The negotiations were not all plain sailing, for Moberly Bell; presumably he was keeping the Walter family fully posted concerning developments, but Bell was not unnaturally very concerned with his own potential situation *vis-à-vis The Times*. He was aware that if Pearson obtained control, he was to be dismissed, but if *The Times* went to Northcliffe, then his future would be secure, so he believed; but one Sunday morning George Sutton arrived with a dispatch case which he allowed Bell to learn contained 'the papers'; his instructions were to hand back these papers unless Bell wrote a letter clarifying the position. Bell wrote the letter.

The first paragraph said that if Northcliffe acquired *The Times*, he, Bell, should act as managing director for five years 'and carry out your absolute instructions'. But Bell had to fight hard for Northcliffe. Sir Alexander Henderson called at Printing House Square and asked Mr Walter whether Northcliffe was the man whose scheme had supplanted Pearson's. Mr Walter's answer was 'No', which shows that although Bell may have kept the Walters informed as to developments in the negotiations, he had not disclosed the name of his patron. Lord Rothschild and Sir Edgar Speyer were also callers on Mr Walter; possibly both were would-be purchasers, but the apparent purpose of their call was to seek information. When Northcliffe's offer of £320,000 was laid before the court, there was opposition from shareholders, but this Northcliffe had anticipated. What interested Northcliffe was the fact that he was ready to pay £400,000 for *The Times* and he obtained it for £320,000. Bell's unsigned cable to him in France, 'Gone through as we wanted', was almost an anti-climax.

Soon after the purchase went through, Northcliffe returned to London and gave a dinner party for some of the members of the editorial staff of *The Times*. One who sat near Northcliffe noticed that he ate little and did not drink more than two glasses of champagne. What the staff did not know was that he had a morbid dislike of eating before strangers, a dislike which naturally applied to public banquets; on these occasions it was usually his custom to eat a hearty meal at home before setting out for the public one. Actually he had a very good appetite indeed. At the time, 1908, when he purchased *The Times* he was accustomed to drink little; later he seemed to feel a need for alcohol. During Prohibition when Northcliffe was in the United States, he drank gin, 'because it looked like water'. Towards the end of his life he drank brandy in some quantities.

At the dinner he gave when he purchased control of *The Times*, Northcliffe astonished the staff in more ways than one; he had each individual member introduced to him separately. Each man was amazed to find how well Northcliffe was posted as to his individual work. Northcliffe had no doubt asked Bell to brief him in this.

Secondly, the staff expected to meet a somewhat uncouth individual. What they saw was a man of forty-three sitting humped up in a chair, loose limbs sprawling; they could not see his eyes for they were hidden behind dark glasses set in the new-fashioned tortoisehell rims. He was quiet—they had been told he was noisy and they were not to know that behind their backs he mocked at them, referred to them as 'Monks' or 'the Brethren'. Perhaps none suspected that North-

cliffe was acting for their benefit; maybe he was not,
but Northcliffe, still to be known as 'Mr X', did not
retain the pose—if pose it was—for very long.

Pearson went to Sicily on holiday after having
talked himself out of the purchasing of *The Times*. The
feud with Northcliffe lasted long, but the breach was
healed before Northcliffe's death. The two men dined
together, and Northcliffe was moved to say that
Pearson's son, the present Sir Nevile Pearson, could
go and work a while in *The Times* office, if he liked!

Although a period of peace settled down in Printing
House Square, it is evident that it was a somewhat
uneasy peace. Evidently, Bell, as happy as he was
because *The Times* now sailed on untroubled financial
waters, feared ructions, so he took good care that 'Mr
X' and Mr Walter did not meet. This was a pity,
because both the Walter brothers resented their
ornamental position, while 'Mr X' was frankly anti-
Walter, but worse was in store.

Mr Wickham Steed was correspondent at Vienna;
he learned indirectly the identity of 'Mr X', and was
appalled; he wrote Bell a frank letter, saying that if
and when the news became known in the highest
circles, many useful doors would be closed to *The
Times* correspondents. Bell showed this letter to Northcliffe, who wrote Steed a very restrained letter, saying
he did not intend interfering with the conduct of *The
Times*, but Bell, usurping editorial prerogatives, and
with or without Northcliffe abetting him, was beginning to send *The Times* correspondents messages
couched in language more generally used at this period
in Carmelite House.

It was not until July 1908, sixteen months after he
obtained control, that Northcliffe first showed his
hand, and showed that despite his protestations that

he would not interfere with the conduct of *The Times*, he did indeed intend to prove who was the master. Mr Hubert Walter, Mr Wickham Steed and Mr Bourchier, *The Times*' famous correspondent in the Balkans, were sent for to appear at the Northcliffe mansion in Surrey, Sutton Place. Northcliffe did not give details, but he made it clear he was meditating editorial changes. Then came the first balance sheet of the new company; it showed a loss. Northcliffe attacked Bell on his methods of keeping accounts, but rarely did he ever approach his subordinates direct; in this case he wrote a letter to Mr Buckle, the Editor, wherein he referred to Bell as 'the old man', and told Buckle he could show Bell the letter, if he liked. Buckle did.

Northcliffe dismissed Kitchin, Bell's assistant, and appointed in his place a personal friend, Mr Reginald Nicolson, of the *Daily Mirror*. Then Northcliffe told Bell he needed a holiday and took him on a three months trip to Newfoundland. Bell found himself nagged all day long and far into the night; he wrote from New York, saying he had to listen to criticism, sneers, slighting allusions and downright abuse.

Bell returned to London to find that in his absence vast changes had been made in the routine of *The Times*. Letters began to fly about; Northcliffe at the end of 1909 wrote the Editor that there must be more changes 'after Christmas'. Northcliffe now dropped the 'Mr X'; he became 'the Chief', as in Carmelite House, and took up residence 'over the shop', living for brief periods in a suite of rooms in Printing House Square.

One Saturday morning, so the story goes, Northcliffe came downstairs arrayed in a top hat and frock coat; walking just in front of him was another top hat and frock coat, their wearer carrying a small black bag. Northcliffe shadowed the man, who appeared to know well where he was going. The man opened a door in a corridor and entered a room and closed the door behind him. A few seconds later, Northcliffe entered the room.

The man was bareheaded now and sitting on a chair, the skirts of his frock coat drawn up over his knees. His hat rested on a table beside the black bag.

'What are you doing in my office?' Northcliffe is said to have demanded.

'Your—I—er—I—er—I don't—I'm doing the same as I do every Saturday morning: the same as I have done every Saturday for the past five and twenty years', the older man is reputed to have replied. Back and forth went question and answer until the matter was cleared up, as follows.

A quarter of a century previously, the Foreign Editor of *The Times* wished to send a member of the staff abroad, but it was a Sunday; there was not sufficient money in the petty cash and no possibility of cashing a cheque. Instructions were given to the bankers, Messrs Coutts, that each and every Saturday a clerk should go to Printing House Square, with the sum of one hundred pounds in golden sovereigns. The clerk was to remain on the premises from Saturday until Monday morning. For a quarter of a century these instructions were faithfully carried out, until Northcliffe intervened and another quaint old custom fell into disuse.

Mr Harcourt Kitchin, the assistant to Moberly Bell who was dismissed, wrote a biography of his former chief wherein he stated: 'He (Northcliffe) told me himself that he did not wish to interfere. "I shall leave the Editor unrestricted control", said he, "unless he should—which is quite impossible—fail to warn the British People of the coming German Peril. I insist upon that duty being discharged." ' But very soon Mr George Buckle, the Editor, was forced to resign; he was replaced by Mr Geoffrey Dawson, who also fell foul of Lord Northcliffe and resigned.

Northcliffe's daily bulletins gave rise to considerable astonishment among members of *The Times* editorial staff. Mr Kitchin voices his astonishment as follows: 'As I watched Lord Northcliffe trying to understand *The Times* and its staff and its readers, and failing to comprehend what its purpose was in the view of those who loved and served it, it was borne upon me . . . the truth that no man can conduct a newspaper who has not himself a mind akin to that of the class of people to whom it is designed to appeal. . . . The English ideas of education as expressed in its public schools and universities may be absurd and effete— nevertheless they are definite and are inspired by a definite purpose. *The Times* had always been a news- paper edited by educated people for educated people —according to its English standards. And no one can understand men and women educated by English standards, unless he himself has been subjected in his youth to the same educational influences. It does not alter a fact to condemn it as the outcome of a caste system to those who do not belong to it. *The Times* was a caste newspaper, and Lord Northcliffe did not belong to that caste. The most appropriate epithet which I can think of to apply to his mind is that which I have already used—it was unfurnished. He had never been educated in the English sense, he had never studied any branch of learning, even perfunctorily, he had never lived on equal terms of mutual criticism with those who had been educated on English lines. This may have been to his pecuniary advantage, but it was a fatal disability for one who sought to influence the conduct of so characteristic an English newspaper as *The Times*. Its ideal were, to him, utterly foreign.'

This devastating summing-up of Northcliffe's personal attitude *vis-à-vis The Times* may be considered unduly harsh, but Mr Kitchin is undoubtedly correct in his insistence on the utterly English characteristics of *The Times*. As an American writer, Quentin Reynolds, once wrote: '*The Times* is as English as a cricket pitch or a bowler hat'.

But Northcliffe, in his own way, was just as English as *The Times*; what then was lacking? where lay his failure—if failure there was—to comprehend the ideals of *The Times*? It has been said—and perhaps unfairly said—that he 'wanted to make *The Times* a threepenny edition of the *Daily Mail*'. Indeed, he did have the idea—and made no attempt to hide it—that *The Times* needed 'gingering up', and he did transfer some members of the *Daily Mail* staff to *The Times* in order to achieve that purpose.

The *History of The Times* has this to say about Northcliffe's relations with the paper:

'From 1912 nothing could dissuade him from trying to use *The Times* as an agency for the promotion of his own personal influence and personal importance. His first "brainstorms", then occasional and slight in their incidence, brought with them a marked degree of megalomania. As early as 1910 there had been whispering that the Chief was not always in his right mind.'

As time went by, Northcliffe found it increasingly difficult to work with *The Times* editorial staff. For instance, he once objected to the French *tant pis* being translated 'so much the worse', and declared that it

EVENINGS IN PRINTING HOUSE SQUARE

Lord Northcliffe : 'Help! Again I feel the demons of sensationalism rising in me.
Hold me fast! Curb me, if you love me!'

(From the original water-colour by the late Sir Max Beerbohm in Printing House Square).

When Lord Northcliffe was embattled with Mr Lloyd George, 'Rip',
famous 'Evening News' cartoonist, pictured them as pugilists surrounded
by well-known characters of the period

'meant Kismet or Fate'. He issued instructions about
the use of the words 'morale' and 'moral', showing
that he did not know how they should be used.

There is, I suggest, much pathos in this record;
Northcliffe striving to great heights, purchasing the
greatest newspaper in the world, and then finding
himself shut out, shut out because of educational
defects; denied entry into a world he wanted to
dominate, but could not. And yet, in the beginning, he
did listen to the advice of Kennedy Jones, who said to
him: 'We don't understand these people [*The Times*
staff]; we don't speak their language. Don't get their
backs up.' But there came a time when Northcliffe
was no longer disposed to hold his horses. Moberly
Bell, the man who had helped him to buy *The Times*,
became a butt for his barbed shafts. Daily telegrams
went to Bell, upbraiding, criticising, until Bell, who
died in harness, became one of those in the opposition
camp.

Northcliffe made no secret of the fact that his
attempt to put *The Times* on a paying basis 'was one
of the toughest propositions in my life'.

The reduction in the selling price of *The Times* was
another 'tough proposition'; an observer records that
in March 1922, Northcliffe was staying at Pau and
had a group of men from his newspapers staying with
him. One guest was Mr Lints-Smith, then manager
of *The Times*; he arrived from London only a few hours
before Northcliffe received an urgent telegram; he
opened and read it and remarked aloud: 'Just as I
thought.' Then he turned to Lints-Smith and said:
'I'm sorry, but you must return to London immediately; the *Daily Telegraph* is coming down to three-halfpence on May 10; *The Times* will be reduced to three-
halfpence for everybody next Monday.' That meant

G

in two days time. For some time previously, *The Times*
was sold to registered readers only for three-halfpence.

Northcliffe then summoned his secretaries and told
them that 'tonight' the *Evening News* must carry the
announcement concerning *The Times*. The news must
be cabled and telephoned and sent to Paris. One
secretary was instructed to telephone to the Mayor of
Pau and the postmaster, and to present Lord Northcliffe's compliments, and say that he had a vital message
which must reach London 'within the next hour or
so'. A message was dictated to the Editor of the
Evening News instructing him to put the announcement
concerning *The Times* in the 'fudge', the newspaper-
language word for 'Stop Press'; a clever touch, that,
stressing the 'newsy' value of what was, after all, but a
shot in an internecine war in Fleet Street. Northcliffe
commented: 'That will shake up the complacent
Elders of *The Times*, that will be the first they will
know of it—reading it in the fudge.' Nothing more was
said until Northcliffe was about to retire, then he told
his guests: 'Wickham Steed (Editor of *The Times*) will
be here tomorrow.'

There one can see Northcliffe in his element; making
mystery and surrounding his genius for organising
with mystery: a boyish sense of mystery, although
Northcliffe was then fifty-seven.

On March 27, when Wickham Steed was seated
next to Bernard Falk, Editor of the *Weekly Dispatch*
(now the *Sunday Dispatch*), Northcliffe tried to start a
a discussion about Jews, but Falk said he would prefer
to talk about the three-halfpenny *Times*. There was a
moment's silence, and then the conversation turned
to the questions of the Arabs in Palestine. Steed
became deeply interested in this subject and spoke
rapidly. Northcliffe, who had kept very quiet, suddenly

broke in: 'But look at that, Steed!'—indicating a poster on the wall. It read:

DAILY TELEGRAPH
1½d. Everywhere
on May 10.

The poster, Northcliffe had obtained from London; it had been so placed opposite Steed that *The Times* Editor could not avoid seeing it every time he looked up from the table. 'That's the thing you have to think about. That's the problem you have to face. . . . Look at it!' When once again the conversation touched upon some problem of high European politics, Northcliffe broke in, growling: 'But look at it. . . . Look at it. Read it. I told you it was coming. That's the fight before you.'

This luncheon party, which took place five months only before Northcliffe died, shows plainly, I suggest, how Northcliffe failed to understand the intricate machine he had purchased. No interest in problems of high European politics which was being discussed at his luncheon table, but an overbearing, blustering attitude towards the Editor of *The Times*, because the Editor was more interested in the editorial content of *The Times* than he was in the selling price of its rival, the *Daily Telegraph*.

In the years following the first World War and until his death in 1922, Lord Northcliffe's interference with the Foreign Service of *The Times* was a long-drawn-out serio-comedy that might well have played irreparable havoc with the world's best-balanced foreign news service. There had been minor matters of interference in the heart of the service, in Printing House Square, but when Northcliffe quarrelled with Lloyd George, the late George Adam, at that time Paris correspondent

of *The Times*, was an innocent victim of the feud
between the Premier and the newspaper proprietor.

Adam had graduated from the business side of
Reuter's Agency and had been a Reuter reporter
before being posted at Paris by *The Times*, which he
served most admirably. Adam was sent to report the
San Remo Conference for *The Times*; Lloyd George
was the chief British delegate. Transmission of cabled
dispatches from San Remo to London was faulty, and
the telephone was not working. Adam was on good
terms with the Premier, with whom he had become
acquainted during the Versailles Peace Conference at
Paris. When the Premier heard of Adam's difficulties,
he offered him the courtesy of the diplomatic valise
which was taken to London every night by a King's
Messenger. It was perhaps not very fair and just to
Adam's newspaper rivals, but down the years *The
Times*' correspondents abroad have become used to
being offered such facilities, such as I myself enjoyed
when I was *The Times*' correspondent at Lisbon.
George Adam could hardly be blamed for accepting
Mr Lloyd George's offer, but Lord Northcliffe did
blame him—and more, he dismissed him forthwith.

Poor Adam! He never recovered from the blow, and
although he secured a number of small appointments,
he spent the rest of his life hoping to be re-instated on
The Times, but he died at a comparatively early age
and in a state of considerable financial embarrassment.

Following on Adam's dismissal, the question arose
of appointing a successor. Whom should it be?

Mr Peter Gouldie was the Editor of the Paris *Daily
Mail*. Gouldie had just settled a strike in the Rue du
Sentier office to Northcliffe's pleasure, and it was to
Gouldie that Northcliffe now turned for advice.

Some little time previously Gouldie had dismissed a

sub-editor for incompetence; his name was Tom
Huddleston and he came from Lancashire to Paris,
where he discarded the 'Tom' and became Sisley
Huddleston. He was a very fat and ungainly man who
looked like a cross between William Shakespeare and
Hall Caine. When he was dismissed from the Paris
Daily Mail, Paris was the news focus of the world
because of the Peace Conference sitting there.
Huddleston, with considerable industry, set about
making himself the Paris correspondent of some twenty
newspapers situated literally all over the world. Part
of his industry was due to a flair for personal advertising; he engaged various famous personages in
wordy warfare and achieved considerable publicity
for himself. So much so, that very possibly Peter
Gouldie wondered whether he had taken the right
step when he dismissed the Lancastrian. In any case,
when Northcliffe asked Gouldie to nominate someone
for the post of Paris correspondent of *The Times*, he
nominated—Sisley Huddleston!

Northcliffe sent a message to Huddleston to meet
him on the Fontainebleau golf links. Huddleston
arrived dressed in his Latin Quarter costume, much to
Northcliffe's delight. 'See that man', said he to Tom
Clarke of the *Daily Mail* who was with him. 'See that
man. Doesn't he look exactly like a foreign correspondent of *The Times*, with that air and hat, and those
clothes!' Then he turned to Huddleston and said:
'Come on, Huddleston, let's see how you walk'.

Northcliffe strode away, with Huddleston waddling
in his wake, and, according to Huddleston himself, he
was engaged as the Paris correspondent of *The Times*
when he was floundering, a non-player, in a bunker.

Despite his carefully prepared bizarre appearance,
the late Sisley Huddleston was very well aware of cash

values, so when Northcliffe asked him how much
money he would ask as a salary for being the Paris
correspondent of the Northcliffian *Thunderer*, Huddleston answered: 'More than it is customary for *The
Times* to pay, my lord'.

Northcliffe had the contract in a side pocket, and
as he played himself out of the bunker, he threw the
contract down at Huddleston's feet and strode away,
leaving the new correspondent to drop his silver-
topped ebony cane and flounder in the sand to pick up
the document.

Sisley Huddleston was engaged for a period of two
years, but it was a stormy passage for him.

The rise and fall of Sisley Huddleston, whose life,
incidentally, was as tragic as that of 'Chief' Northcliffe,
could well be regarded as a signpost pointing to the
mental deterioration of the proprietor of *The Times*,
which, in all probability, began long before that
famous encounter on Fontainebleau golf links. Ferdinand Tuohy, another of Northcliffe's favourites, whose
career was cut off in mid-air, so to speak, said of Sisley
Huddleston, that he always wrote with Adelphic
flatulency, while Huddleston's predecessor, George
Adam, told him he was like a cod served *en furie*: he
always had his tale in his mouth. Huddleston bore no
malice against those amiable insults but continued to
live in his apartment in the Latin Quarter, where he
was understood to have married his secretary. He had
large Frenchified visiting cards engraved with the
words:

'Sisley Huddleston et Madame.'

Huddleston was summoned to accompany Northcliffe and Wickham Steed from Paris to Geneva. In a
first-class railway compartment the Paris correspondent
sat opposite the Chief, who regarded him with malevo-

lence, and then began to address him as follows: 'Your finger-nails are dirty, Huddleston—and your clothes! They are awful! Go to my tailor and get yourself a decent suit of clothes.'

Huddleston rose with bulky dignity. 'I allow no one to criticise my clothes, my lord, but as they appear to displease you, allow me to retire'—which he did. He stayed in the corridor until the train reached the next stopping place, where he alighted and returned to Paris.

Huddleston worked for *The Times* until his contract expired. It was not renewed.

The ex-Paris correspondent of *The Times* lived in his mill in Normandy until the outbreak of war, but fearful of the German advance, he moved away to Monte Carlo, where he stayed until the fall of France. Then he became an active collaborator with the Germans.

Huddleston became a French citizen and toured France under German auspices, lecturing and attacking Britain and the United States.

When Germany surrendered, Huddleston was arrested and put on trial by the Free French. He might have been given the death sentence—he was a French subject—or most certainly a severe prison sentence for treason, but a former colleague, an American correspondent and now an officer in the U.S.A. Army, made a dramatic last-moment intervention on the prisoner's behalf. Huddleston was, with a contemptuous gesture, acquitted.

When Huddleston died, in 1951, the man who had wafted him to dizzy heights had already been dead for nearly thirty years.

ONE of the most popular Northcliffe legends pictures him as the man who foretold the first World War; the man who did more than any other man to win it, and in the winning of it put Asquith out of office and Lloyd George in. Combined with this legend there is, of course, the story of how Northcliffe drove Kitchener from the War Office during the course of a campaign known as the 'Shell Shortage Scandal'. At different times, different people have registered their own first-hand impressions of the events which form part of this Northcliffe legend, but the facts pieced together make a picture that gives the lie to the legend.

Throughout his life Northcliffe retained a boyish enthusiasm for stories of adventure; it might be called a G. A. Henty mind. One did not have to take the stories seriously, but Northcliffe was apt from time to time to play mental leap-frog, to jump from a story that had began as entertainment and alight on some amazing and not always logical conclusion. One has seen how much the Chief liked stories about the invasion of Britain. It has all been good reader entertainment, but when the first World War broke on the world, Northcliffe took his own created 'invasion scare' very seriously; it caused ructions in Carmelite

House, and narrowly avoided upsetting Britain in the first hours of the war.

What is the basis for the claim that Northcliffe knew the war was coming? True, he has often been pilloried —and I think most unfairly—as a 'warmonger'. I can find no reason why. True again, he boosted the Territorial Army, but the Liberal Government of the day wanted the Territorial Army boosted. Northcliffe boosted the play, *An Englishman's Home*, which was a 'war' play, but Northcliffe also boosted the religious play *The Miracle* and nobody would claim that Northcliffe was boosting religion. Did Northcliffe really realise that war was coming? Perhaps he did, perhaps he did not, but one thing is certain; when it did come he did not understand the importance of it!

This particular story begins in the Spring of 1914. The world went pretty well then. The only big head-lines in the British newspapers were concerned with the prospect of civil war in Ireland. We find North-cliffe at this period acting somewhat queerly; I think in view of what happened—and more particularly in view of what might have happened if Northcliffe had had his own way—it is just as well if we examine Northcliffe's methods and movements at this period particularly closely. Northcliffe was sending daily cables of criticism at full rates. At this time also, according to a high-level authority in Carmelite House, Northcliffe wanted to make *The Times* a halfpenny and literally had to be physically restrained!

On Sunday, June 28, 1914, the Archduke Ferdinand was assassinated at Sarajevo, in Serbia. Northcliffe certainly did not recognise this as a danger signal, any more than the majority of people, because a month later he was sending messages to Carmelite House patting himself on the back for having obtained a

scoop about the King's decision to summon a conference of the leaders of all parties on the subject of
Ulster. Five days later the war started.

When Britain was on the verge of war, Northcliffe
was in Ireland. He returned to London on July 31st
and on Saturday, August 1st, attended an editorial
conference in *The Times* office. Northcliffe told the
Editors of *The Times* and *Daily Mail* that, according
to his information, the British Government was not
prepared to stand by France and Russia, because
certain financial interests were at work to keep Britain
neutral. He seemed inclined to the belief that these
influences might prevail; he asked aloud what attitude
his newspapers should adopt if this happened.
Wickham Steed, then Foreign Editor of *The Times*,
immediately opted for an attack on the Government.
Thomas Marlowe, Editor of the *Daily Mail*, took the
opposite view. He said that an attack on the Government in a moment of national crisis would be un-
forgivable. Northcliffe himself was undecided. He
remarked that there was much to be said for both
points of view and adjourned the conference for
twenty-four hours. When the men met the next afternoon, Germany was about to invade Belgium. Three
days later, Wednesday, August 5, Great Britain had
declared war on Germany, but still Northcliffe did not
understand. He flew into a violent temper and created
a scene about the plans for a British Expeditionary
Force for France. To the amazement of the editorial
conference, he declared vehemently that he was quite
opposed to sending British soldiers to France.

'What is this I hear', he cried, 'about a British
Expeditionary Force for France? It is nonsense. Not a
single soldier shall leave this country. We have a
superb Fleet, which shall give all the assistance in its

power, but I will not support the sending out of this country of a single British soldier. What about invasion? What about our own country? Put that in the leader. Do you hear? Not a single soldier will go with my consent. Say so in the paper tomorrow.'

Let us dwell for a moment on this amazing outburst. What would readers of the *Daily Mail* have thought, what would Britain have thought, if Northcliffe's orders had been obeyed? Fortunately for Northcliffe's reputation and prestige in the country and overseas, his orders were not obeyed. It cannot truly be said that, in the words of the French proverb, 'the night brings counsel'. Something entirely different happened.

Thomas Marlowe, great editor, great patriot and great man, 'stood up' to the Chief—and won! It was the most dramatic night in the history of the *Daily Mail*; likely enough the most dramatic night in the life of any British newspaper. It was truly a case of the Editor's decision being final. That *cliché* became a great truism on the night of Wednesday, August 5, 1914.

Northcliffe wrote a leading article saying that no British troops should be sent overseas. Marlowe wrote a leading article supporting the dispatch of a British Expeditionary Force. Both leading articles were set in type: they came back in column proof, were corrected by their respective authors and went back to the printers and were set for page proofs. Northcliffe was now at Printing House Square, in *The Times* office, and Marlowe was in Carmelite House. The printers were waiting to be told which page was to go into tomorrow's paper. Marlowe went to the Head Printer of the *Daily Mail* and told him that neither page was to go into the paper until he himself gave permission.

There were telephone conversations between Carmelite House and Printing House Square. Finally the *Daily Mail* went to press forty-five minutes late, but it was with the Marlowe leader.

What pressure was brought to bear on Northcliffe? Could it have been that once again he was 'physically restrained'? Is the story true that a certain member of the Asquith Cabinet went in person to *The Times* office that night? If so, did he go at Marlowe's instigation? The answer to that question we shall never know. Northcliffe never made any reference to that fateful night, and neither did Marlowe.

So, Northcliffe, willy-nilly, went to war. Once in the war, he, as he had every right to do, made 'talking points' out of it and did everything possible to see that his readers obtained the best possible war news service. Northcliffe cared little for 'fine writing', although he wanted his reporters and special correspondents to write vividly, and they did, but above all he wanted facts. First the facts and then the whys and wherefores. In his quest for 'talking points' in the early days of the war, Northcliffe wanted Kitchener to go to the War Office. Asquith, the Prime Minister, had taken temporary charge, but it was known that Asquith wanted to put Lord Haldane back there. Northcliffe had other ideas. All his life he had applied this method to his newspaper business: 'Get an expert to write it'. A golfer to write about golf; a clergyman to write about religion; a Jew to write about Jewish matters. Now here was a war; therefore, soldiers should be in charge. Kitchener should go to the War Office; besides, there was reader-interest in such an appointment. Kitchener was a name for the masses to conjure with: 'Kitchener of Khartoum'; Kitchener the 'strong silent Englishman'. Asquith did not want

Kitchener at the War Office, and according to Sir George Arthur, who was Kitchener's secretary, Kitchener did not want to go to the War Office. In the light of later events, it is important to remember this.

According to Sir George Arthur, Kitchener was going to return to his post in Egypt. Sir George submits evidence of this, but, says Sir George, it was not difficult for Northcliffe to impose his will on Asquith. Kitchener did not listen; he went ahead with his plans and was actually on board a Channel steamer when a messenger arrived with an order that he was to return immediately to London. Kitchener, the man who less than a year later Northcliffe was to refer to contemptuously as 'a tall man with a narrow forehead', agreed to take over the War Office as a temporary job.

Northcliffe personally organised the sending out of a corps of correspondents to the Western Front, but Kitchener would not allow any journalist anywhere near the seat of any action. Now Northcliffe was in direct conflict with Kitchener. What was this man doing? Did he not know that he, Northcliffe, was the man who had placed him in power? Northcliffe the journalist knew the importance of 'telling the public about the war'. It was their war and they had every right to know what was going on. In vain Northcliffe pointed out what the Germans were doing to publicise *their* war, but Kitchener was adamant. Northcliffe had boosted Kitchener, and Kitchener was the most popular figure in Britain. What to do?

The *Daily Mail* published an emotional story by Hamilton Fyfe about the Retreat from Mons. The opening sentence of the dispatch read: 'Would to God I had not to tell this story. . . .' The country was plunged into gloom. F. E. Smith (later Lord Birkenhead) was the Chief Censor and had passed the dispatch, but the Government issued an official *communiqué* insinuating that the *Daily Mail* had exaggerated the facts. F. E. Smith wrote a private and confidential letter to the Editor of the *Daily Mail* saying that the facts were correct. Northcliffe obtained the letter and ordered that it should be published. His attention was called to the private nature of it, but he insisted it should be published. It was published.

How well informed was Northcliffe during those war years? Here is one of his own statements made in October 1914. 'I have seen the Government, and they asked me to work up a strong recruiting campaign. I declined point-blank, until our men (his war correspondents) are treated properly, and facilities given them to help recruiting by telling about our army. I can get half-a-million men, but I must do it my own way. They would not agree, so I refused point-blank. They want more vigour, more imagination, more organisation.' This may all have been very true, but this self-picture of Northcliffe does not exhibit him in a very patriotic light. It came down to this: if Northcliffe's correspondents were not allowed to report the war, well, he was not going to play. The nation needs recruits. Too bad; I will get them for you in my own way, or not at all. The talk of the need of vigour, imagination and organisation did not make sense. Those words did not belong to the argument at all. The Government had taken Northcliffe into its confidence, but he did not react. It was probably the first time since the outbreak of war that the Government had done so. I base this assumption on a statement by Ferdinand Tuohy, who at the outbreak of war was a *Daily Mail* war correspondent.

In October 1914, Northcliffe sent for Tuohy and

said to him: 'Young man, you have the chance of your life. The British Fleet is going to cover a landing on the Belgium coast. There may be a big naval battle—our first real one since Trafalgar. You are to report this for my papers. You'll find a yacht . . . the Darling something . . . down at Dover. I've bought her. She's mine. Sail straight away and, mind, keep as near the battle as you can. I want a first-class eye-witness account.'

Actually the 'Darling something' was the 'Grace Darling', named after the famous British heroine of whom Northcliffe seemed not to have heard. The 'yacht' was in point of fact a small motor yacht. The late Ferdinand Tuohy and the late Christopher Lumsby of *The Times* duly obeyed Northcliffe's orders and set out on this ridiculous expedition. It was indeed ridiculous; a naval battle and a landing on the Belgian coast! From whom had Northcliffe received his information? Naturally, what Tuohy called a 'Northcliffe conception' never materialised. The two correspondents were constantly hailed by British patrol craft and ordered through megaphones to explain their business. The reply was always the same; that they were taking a supply of chloroform to the Queen of the Belgians' Hospital at Furnes.

For two days and nights the 'Grace Darling' journeyed in the waters between England and Belgium; then the motor yacht lost her rudder and was towed by a British cruiser into Dunkirk. So ended the Northcliffe 'expedition', a serio-comic affair, which even at this moment leaves one wondering what it all meant.

Numerous correspondents, including the present writer, had strange experiences trying to penetrate the fog of war. I was present at the Battle of the Marne,

which I saw as a prisoner of war—a prisoner, I may
say, of my own people. I was 'captured' and held by
the British 4th Division. With me was a *Daily Mail*
correspondent, a Mr Baggs, of whom I have never
heard since those sunny September days, when Major-
General Snow's Staff discussed perfectly seriously
whether we were to be shot or kept in the Cherche-
Midi Prison, Paris, 'for the duration'. We were handed
over to the French police, who were told we were to
go to prison, but the police released us as soon as we
were taken to Paris.

In December 1914, Northcliffe evidently thought it
necessary to justify his claim that he had in his newspaper foretold the war. He had compiled a volume
entitled: 'Scaremongerings from the *Daily Mail*: 1906-
1914'.

The title, of course, was intended to be 'writ
sarcastic'. The publication was a bitter attack on
Liberal newspapers, which Northcliffe referred to as
the 'Hide-the-Truth Press'. The *Star* in a leading
article made this reply: 'Next to the Kaiser, Lord
Northcliffe has done more than any living man to
bring about the war'. This, naturally, was an oblique
justification, a qualification of what Northcliffe called
prophecy, meaning that his newspapers had created a
war atmosphere.

In April, 1915, Northcliffe went to France to visit
the Front. He brought back with him a large German
shell which he had conveyed to the *Daily Mail* office
in a taxi-cab. Northcliffe had the shell placed in the
ante-room of his private office and then summoned
the editorial and business executives to come and see
it. He called their attention to the trophy, giving a
graphic account of its potential dangers. If the shell
exploded, he said, it would traverse the ceiling above

it; above that ceiling Andrew Caird would be sitting. Caird, the controller of finances, was at that moment looking at the shell with some anxiety.

When Northcliffe left, Caird had the shell removed to a Territorial Artillery unit headquarters to be examined. The ten-inch German shell had been reconstructed from odd parts and was quite harmless, but they never told Northcliffe. A few days later Northcliffe did indeed launch a live shell; the echo of its explosion may still be heard.

In the summer of 1914, Northcliffe in the *Daily Mail* had cried: 'The Nation calls for Lord Kitchener!'

Nine months after boosting Kitchener into the War Office, Northcliffe in the *Daily Mail* cried: 'Kitchener Must Go!' Why was this call? Was it because Kitchener still refused to allow the Northcliffe correspondents—and, of course, others as well—to report the war? Naturally, Northcliffe did not give this as the reason for his campaign. The campaign's alleged reason was a shortage of shells, and the shortage was said to be due to the inefficiency of Kitchener.

Lord French was then in command of the British Army in France. French, like Redvers Buller in the Boer War, was a heavy drinker; stories of his drinking drifted back to London. Northcliffe at this time was a staunch supporter of French, chiefly because French was on bad terms with Kitchener. Something had to be done to unseat Kitchener, but what reason could be given to the country? French went to England on leave, where it was understood that he spent a few days with Northcliffe at Elmwood, his home in Thanet. Previous to this leave, there had been stories in Fleet Street of an alleged shortage of shells, but nothing was published in any newspaper. What Northcliffe really had in his mind one cannot be sure, because he always

H

went off at tangents. For instance, in the same week
of May 1915 that he launched his attack on Kitchener,
we find Northcliffe launching—and immediately
stopping—a campaign to use poison gas against the
Germans. This provided the Germans with excellent
propaganda. Later, after a visit to the French front at
Verdun, which played a part in the 1914-18 war
similar to Stalingrad in the 1939-45 war, Northcliffe
wrote in a dispatch that the Germans went into battle
'doped' with ether. This was quite untrue. I mention
these Northcliffe war dispatches in this sequence so
that they shall be read in relationship to his 'Kitchener
Must Go' campaign.

The attack on Kitchener began with the Fleet
Street whispering campaign; then, on May 14,
Northcliffe's *Times* published a dispatch from its
correspondent, Colonel Repington, at French's Headquarters. In this dispatch the Colonel affirmed that
the British advance at Ypres had been held up owing
to the shortage of high-explosive shells. There never
was and never has been any suggestion that this dispatch was other than a reporting of facts, but it was
said during the eventual controversy that General
French himself had initialled the dispatch, which
meant that it would pass the Censors.

The next step in the 'Kitchener Must Go' campaign
was the publication in the *Daily Mail* on May 21, a
week after the first gun had been fired in *The Times*,
of a smashing attack on Kitchener; very cleverly
Northcliffe linked his 'shell shortage' story to a crisis
in the Cabinet. Some years ago Lord Beaverbrook
wrote and published a book, *Politicians and the Press*,
wherein he gives the whole of the inside story of the
Cabinet crisis which led to the downfall of the Asquith
Government and the installation of the first Coalition

Government. Beaverbrook makes it perfectly clear that the shortage of shells had nothing whatsoever to do with the downfall of Asquith, for which Northcliffe gave himself full credit. Beaverbrook shows that Northcliffe had not been aware of what was transpiring in the innermost political circles in Britain. Actually, the Liberal Government's downfall was due to the quarrel between Winston Churchill, then First Lord of the Admiralty, and Lord Fisher, the First Sea Lord. Beaverbrook affirms that the Liberal Government was finished on May 17, which was *five days before* Northcliffe launched his campaign in the *Daily Mail* alleging that 'Lord Kitchener's grave error' had caused a crisis in the Government.

The people of Britain, Britons overseas, foreigners in their own countries all were stunned, shocked beyond measure at this attack on Kitchener. The reader-reaction was tremendous; people cancelled their orders for the supply of the *Daily Mail*; telegrams, letters and cables poured into Carmelite House. On the London Stock Exchange there was an anti-Northcliffe demonstration during which copies of the *Daily Mail* were burned. Sir Max Pemberton, giving his account of this demonstration, said: 'The *Daily Mail* was burned by Germans on the Stock Exchange', but he does not say or attempt to explain what the Germans were doing on the London Stock Exchange during a war in which their country was engaged with Great Britain, or why Germans should be so angry that Kitchener, Britain's greatest hero, should be attacked by the proprietor of Britain's newspaper with the largest circulation. The only place in the world where any glee was caused by the Northcliffe attack on Kitchener was, of course, in Germany.

Some alarm was caused in Carmelite House by the

public outcry; a telephone message was sent to Scotland Yard asking for special police protection for the building. All doors leading to the street were locked. The editorial executives waited for Northcliffe. At five p.m. he appeared. He was wearing a blue suit and a green slouch hat, it is recorded, and he was chewing the end of a big cigar. He dropped into an easy chair exclaiming: 'I have thrown off another string of pearls for you today'. When he was shown the London evening newspapers, which, with the exception of his own *Evening News*, attacked him, he crunched them up and threw them on the floor, saying: 'That shows they don't know the truth. Why, even today General French has told Asquith that if things don't improve he will leave his job to come to England and stump the country, to acquaint the people with the true state of affairs at the Front.'

This terrible statement has never been challenged, but if, as Northcliffe said, the London newspapers 'did not know the truth', it shows that Northcliffe himself was not acquainted with it, or, he did not know what he did not want to know; the one or the other. On May 17, Bonar Law had formally agreed to take part in a Coalition Government, so what use was it for French to write a threatening letter to Asquith on May 21? If French had 'left his job' he would not have been allowed to 'stump the country' because he would have been placed under arrest.

Northcliffe said during the beginning of his Kitchener campaign that he did not care whether as a result of it the circulation of *The Times* fell to one copy and the circulation of the *Daily Mail* to two. Several of Northcliffe's biographers have written reams about the great risks Northcliffe ran with his Kitchener campaign and the huge losses he sustained, but let us

look at the figures. Northcliffe himself remarked at this
time: 'We are getting a lot of free advertising from
competing newspapers'. In point of fact, the Kitchener
attack cost the *Daily Mail* some 60,000 papers, but a
few weeks previously it had put on 100,000.

Northcliffe was very keen that his rivals should
publish their net sales when he published the net sales
of the *Daily Mail*. In 1916, the year of the attack on
Kitchener, the average daily net sale of the *Daily Mail*
was 1,172,245. In 1917, the figure dropped well below
the million mark; the average daily net sale was
938,211, but in 1918, the average net daily circulation
began to climb again. Whether this drop in circulation
was due to the attack on Kitchener, there is no way of
knowing, but even if this temporary set-back was due
to the clamour, the drop did not mean any reduction
in advertising rates, thus it incurred no financial loss.
The falling off in circulation, in fact, calls for but one
piece of comment: if, as Northcliffe maintained, his
campaign was justified and the ends justified the
means, then this justification was not reflected in the
quick return of readers. It took two years for the circulation of Northcliffe's favourite organ to pick up again.
He did not drive Kitchener out of office; a Ministry
of Munitions was set up, Lloyd George became the
Minister; but this was not a result of the 'Kitchener
Must Go' campaign any more than Asquith's departure from office was.

Although Northcliffe always disclaimed he had any
vendetta with any British statesman, his first clash
with one—Asquith—certainly showed a very bitter
feeling, for he gave personal instructions in Carmelite
House that only the worst possible photographs of
Asquith were to be used.

Another politician whom Northcliffe could not abide

was Earl Curzon; yet another was Lord Derby. Curzon
had a Jewish grandmother; that alone was sufficient
to damn him in Northcliffe's eyes, but the Chief went
further: he said that Curzon's real name was Cohen.
Lord Derby, a well-nourished gentleman, was, in
Northcliffe's private code, 'The Fat Man'. This
mystery code was copied by some of Northcliffe's
minor satellites. Northcliffe had a correspondent in
Paris named Harold Cardoza. I, at that time, had an
office in the *Matin* building, the façade of which was
painted red; so I, in the Cardoza–*Daily Mail* code,
was: 'The man in the Red House'.

With the departure of Asquith, Northcliffe looked
around for somebody to boost in his place. For a little
while he thought of Mr Hughes, the deaf Prime
Minister of Australia, but he did not follow through
with that idea. Lloyd George became Premier and
Lloyd George became, for a while, the Northcliffe
blue-eyed boy. This lasted until Lloyd George told
Northcliffe bluntly to 'go to hell'.

It was an uneasy friendship. It began well enough;
Northcliffe gave Lloyd George much support in his
newspapers, but in 1917, only a year after Lloyd
George had taken office, we find the Premier asking
Northcliffe to head a mission to the United States.
Northcliffe did a splendid job there, but naturally,
during the period he was in Government service,
Northcliffe had to abandon the personal control of his
newspaper; one cannot help wondering whether this
was not something of a relief to Lloyd George. At a
later stage in that war the name of Lord Beaverbrook
was being mentioned as a prospective Governor of
Canada. I met him in Paris and asked him if the report
was true. He laughed and said: 'Lloyd George won't
get rid of *me* as easily as that!'

Whether Lloyd George meant to muzzle Northcliffe by giving him a seat in the Government must be a matter of opinion, but when, in 1917, Northcliffe returned to London from Washington, his Government job ended, Lloyd George was furiously angry, not because Northcliffe refused it, but because of the manner in which he did. Lord Cowdray was head of the Air Office and expected to be made Minister. Lloyd George did not tell him that he was offering the post to Northcliffe. Northcliffe wrote Lloyd George a letter on November 15, 1917, and published the letter immediately he wrote it. Through the published letter, Lord Cowdray received the first intimation that he had been by-passed. Still more, in the first paragraph of his letter, Northcliffe declined the offer, but the rest of the long letter was an attack on the Lloyd George administration, also its conduct of the war. Nevertheless, Lloyd George made two further attempts to rope in Northcliffe, but with these, the offer of the War Office and the appointment as Director of Propaganda against Enemy Countries I have dealt elsewhere in this book.

Lloyd George committed to paper his estimation and appreciation of Northcliffe's qualities. Firstly, he approved Northcliffe's contention that an editor of a great London newspaper was better informed about events happening in the world's capitals than any Cabinet Minister. Northcliffe said and Lloyd George agreed that the information that reached the Cabinet was 'carefully filtered'.

On the other hand, Lloyd George agreed with Beaverbrook that Northcliffe knew nothing about his (Lloyd George's) consultations with Bonar Law and Lord Carson, negotiations to which I have already referred, and which preceded the retirement of

Asquith. Lloyd George went further; he added, a little
maliciously perhaps: 'when he (Northcliffe) saw that
something was going on, he made an effort to resume
friendly relations'. According to Lloyd George, Northcliffe was not only left out, but he was not, so far as
Lloyd George knew, even informed as to what was
actually taking place. Lloyd George was bitter about
Northcliffe's threats to attack him in his newspapers,
if he (Lloyd George) 'continued to interfere with the
soldiers'. Further remarks of Lloyd George, however,
show that he had every reason for bitterness; the
former Premier says that Northcliffe was the 'kettle-
drum of Sir Douglas Haig'! As one reads through the
files of the Northcliffe newspapers of the period, one
realises only too well that Northcliffe, at long last,
learning that French's feet were clay, set up Haig in
his place and banged the drums and sounded the
brass to tell all and sundry that Haig was sacrosanct;
that all who dared to criticise him were intriguers and
should be ousted. Unhappily, in the end, *The Times*
speaking with the subdued voice of Northcliffe was
forced to acknowledge that Haig's humanity was
fringed with his errors. The victories Haig could not
win in Flanders, Northcliffe helped him to win in
Fleet Street. But so with Haig, so with the Frenchman
Joffre. The French critics of Joffre complained that
he was always winning the Battle of the Marne.
Northcliffe's *dicta*, that editors of great London
journals were better informed than Cabinet Ministers,
is not true if the editors are as Lloyd George described
Northcliffe. '. . . was characteristic of Lord Northcliffe's
worst side. It was what made it so difficult to have
confidential dealings with him. Where either his vanity
or temper was implicated, he had no regard for the
decent behaviour which bound the average man of

honour.' This was written in comment on the story I have already related of how Northcliffe refused the portfolio of the Air Ministry.

In Bernard Falk's autobiography, he mentions a report that Northcliffe was to be made Viceroy of Ireland, 'because he was Irish-born'. We have seen that he was, but he left Ireland as a babe-in-arms. Northcliffe dismissed the report with a shrug, saying that the post was but an empty one. Northcliffe, nevertheless, at the beginning of the first World War, told his associates that if the Irish problem was turned over to him, he could solve it. Actually, his scheme was the same as the one eventually adopted: partition. Agreed that it was the obvious solution and that Northcliffe's scheme was like the story of Christopher Columbus and the egg, it *was* the eventual solution taken by the British Government of the day, but this method of direct action, which Lloyd George likened to dictatorial power: would it have proved serviceable to Britain if Northcliffe had been given the wartime powers he wanted?

Falk's autobiography shows him to be among those who believed that Northcliffe was on the inside of things, and he writes much in direct contradiction to what Lloyd George has to say in his own memoirs. For instance, Falk writes that Northcliffe was 'well apprised (December 1916) of the development in the swiftly changing scene' and (*apropos* Asquith): 'they have got the old man down at last.'

Writing in his diary of the same period, Mr Tom Clarke says (December 11, 1916): 'He (Northcliffe) says there is a plot against L.G.; that it should be shown up'.

Obviously, Northcliffe must have believed himself to be—whether he was or not—on very close terms

with Lloyd George, because, on the night of the day
the quoted diary entry is made, we find Northcliffe
telephoning to his News Editor to say: 'Ring up Lloyd
George and ask him (in relation to some political point
the News Editor did not understand). Give him my
compliments and tell him I told you to. Ring him up
any time on vital matters.' Rather a curious mentality,
one may think, telling a subordinate to ring up a wartime Premier of Great Britain and ask him to explain
a point in obscurity. Two days after these instructions,
we find Northcliffe demanding the requisitioning of
the Royal Automobile Club. Whether this was or was
not a 'vital matter' is not explained, but we learn that
Northcliffe did not approve of the Club's magnificent
swimming-baths.

Northcliffe told Falk that whenever the Premier's
secretaries saw Northcliffe's top hat coming round the
corner of Downing Street, they took fright, and he
added that when he (Northcliffe) went to 10 Downing
Street on a matter of importance, Lloyd George did
not hesitate to leave a meeting of the Cabinet. Falk
comments that this possibly was exaggeration.

With regard to both the short-term wartime posts
Northcliffe occupied, the first as head of a mission to
the United States, and the second as Director of
Propaganda against Enemy Countries, Lloyd George
was fully appreciative of the services Northcliffe
rendered, although with regard to the first post, Lloyd
George places some stress on the criticism of Northcliffe both at home and in the United States. With
regard to the second post, Lloyd George has this to
say: 'It (the propaganda) was done with great skill
and subtlety. The credit for its success is due to Lord
Beaverbrook and Lord Northcliffe.'

Beaverbrook was junior to Northcliffe. Was it by

accident or design that Lloyd George placed Beaverbrook's name first in the credit line? Both Beaverbrook
and Lloyd George were in agreement as to Northcliffe's power and influence—or the lack of it—in
political circles during the war years, but both Bernard
Falk and Tom Clarke, who were in Northcliffe's
employment during those critical periods, stress the
alleged power. Which of the two pairs is right? Perhaps
the truth is to be found somewhere between those two
opposed points of view. But outside of politics there
were other things: the 'shell shortage' and the violent
anti-Kitchener campaign in which Northcliffe was the
animateur and leading figure. Did this help or hinder
the winning of the war?

As a tailpiece to this controversy, I would add only
what Lloyd George had to say to Tom Clarke, after
Northcliffe's death: 'When Northcliffe asked me to
put him on the Peace Delegation (Paris 1919) I told
him to go to hell. I broke with Northcliffe. I refused
absolutely to have him at the Peace Conference. I put
up with him for four years. The break had to come—
when he wanted to dictate to me. As Prime Minister
I could not allow that. It was a good thing for me that
I did not get turned out while he was alive, or he
would have claimed that he had done it!'

CHAPTER VII

The Noise and the People

IN the British newspaper world it is affirmed that Northcliffe boosted the wages of newspapermen: certainly there is a hard core of truth in this statement, but, nevertheless, the statement should not stand by itself. It was Northcliffe the newspaper proprietor who began the policy of buying men from rival newspapers, and in the newspaper business, as in all businesses for the matter of that, money is the carrot dangled in front of the person whose allegiance is to be seduced. Notwithstanding, Northcliffe did, in the by and large, pay good salaries, but according to one of his close associates for many years, the reason why Northcliffe paid so well was that he knew the things which mattered and those which did not; among the things he considered to be without importance were leading articles. On the other hand, he knew what the mass of newspaper readers wanted, and he gave it to them; Northcliffe frankly appealed to the many and not to the intellegent few.

But Northcliffe was by no means a cynic in this respect; he had no contempt for the tastes of his readers, but because on the whole he had more sympathy for them than with the others, he gave them what they wanted. What he himself wanted was to increase the circulation of his publications.

Yet he played skilfully on the snobbishness of certain men and women. He knew that they liked to believe that the paper which they read was read by 'the best people'. His object all sublime was to make his advertisers believe this, too, so that they would compete eagerly for space and willingly pay high rates for their privileges.

It was Northcliffe's aim to persuade his readers that the *Daily Mail* did everything on the grand scale. The aforementioned close associate summed up: 'He liked stories to be told of the large salaries it could afford to pay. Northcliffe expected his editorial staff to assist in creating the impression that his newspapers treated them in a princely way.'

But another close associate, Tom Clarke, had this comment to make on this 'princely way'. He said: 'An outburst of generosity by the Chief on one's behalf generally meant a subsequent unpleasant half-hour with Caird' (the keeper of the money-bags).

Caird (who later became Sir Andrew Caird) was the man who had to pass the reporters' expense accounts. In the *Daily Mail* office they used to tell this story about Caird and one of the *Daily Mail* star reporters. It was said that Charles Hands, the reporter in this story, made a bet with some colleagues. Hands affirmed that Caird only looked at the total of an expense account, never at the items. He bet that he could 'get away' with anything in an expense account, provided that the questionable item was buried in the body of the account. The bet was taken and, so the story goes, Hands 'got away' with the item: 'To hansom cab, up and down office stairs . . . 2s. 6d.'

When Queen Victoria was dying at Osborne,

Hands was what they call in newspaper offices 'the death watch'. His functions were to dispatch daily reports and to send the story of the last scenes the moment the Queen died. The news agencies flashed the news of the death of the Queen, now the office waited on Hands' story, but it did not arrive. A junior was rushed to Hands' hotel to see what the trouble was. The brilliant reporter—and he was a brilliant reporter according to all accounts—was found in tears, surrounded by sheets and sheets of paper. The young reporter picked up a handful and found that on each sheet there was but a fragment of a sentence; every fragment was the same. It started: 'Never since the death of Jesus Christ . . .'

Hands was the hero of many stories; most of them were concerned with the 'sack'. Many Northcliffe stories are concerned with dismissal or threats of dismissal. Once, so it is said, when Hands had been threatened with the 'sack', the door of Northcliffe's office in the *Daily Mail* opened and Hands crawled in on his hands and knees, whispering: 'Is it safe now, Chief?'

Another time when the threat of dismissal was hanging over Hands' head, he took his small son to the *Daily Mail* office, waited until Northcliffe appeared, then drew his son's attention to Northcliffe, saying very audibly: 'That's the kind gentleman, my boy, who buys all your lovely suits'. When that small boy grew up, Northcliffe paid for his education at Cambridge. When Hands' eyesight began to fail, he was pensioned. He died, quite blind.

The late James Dunn was another of the old-time 'star' reporters of the *Daily Mail*, and, like Hands, the hero of many stories. Incidentally, Dunn was supposed to bear a strong physical likeness to the Chief, a fact

which caused junior members of the staff to rush for
cover each time Dunn was sighted in a corridor; such
was the awe inspired by the appearance of the Chief—
or his double!

The stories of James Dunn—'Jimmy' Dunn to Fleet
Street—are many, so it is perhaps inevitable that the
best one concerning a certain episode in Birmingham
has become somewhat embellished with the passage of
time. Yet, *ben trovato* or no, it is I think, worth the
telling.

Northcliffe's sense of humour was something like
Dickens' Mr Squeers: 'How d'you spell winders?
Well, go and clean 'em!' Northcliffe, having heard
that Dunn had been having a gay spell, ordered that
he should go to Birmingham to report the annual
meeting of the British Temperance Society, which was
to open on the following Monday. 'Now, Jimmy', said
the News Editor of the *Daily Mail*, 'you start off tomorrow, Saturday, that will give you a day's rest.'
Dunn drew the money for his expenses and left for
Birmingham.

On Sunday afternoon the telephone rang in the
News Editor's room. 'This is Dunn speaking', said a
voice. 'Get me a shorthand writer; I've got a grand
story. Snakes are crawling up the pillars of Corpora-
tion Street Station; lions . . .'

'Cut that out, Jimmy', snapped the News Editor.
'Get to bed.' He hung up.

Half an hour later the telephone tinkled again.
'Why did you cut me off?' enquired Dunn plaintively.
'Get this story: lions and tigers are roaming round the
station. Snakes. . . .'

'For God's sake, Jimmy, get some sleep', pleaded
the News Editor, 'otherwise I'll have to report you to
the Chief. Get to bed!' And again he hung up.

About seven o'clock there was another telephone
call from Birmingham. This time it was the late Harold
Pemberton (son of Sir Max Pemberton), then Motoring Correspondent of the *Daily Mail*. This is what
Harold Pemberton had to say. 'I'm on my way to the
Motor Show in Coventry', he stated. 'I happened to
run into Jimmy Dunn here in Birmingham. He's in
tears; he says he has a grand story and you won't take
it. Bostock's Menagerie train was wrecked in Corpor-
ation Street Station this afternoon.'

It is strange but true that the policy of a newspaper
seems to place its imprint on the personality of their
staffs. For instance, the old *Daily News* which Northcliffe always referred to as the 'Cocoa Press'—because
it belonged to the Cadbury family—had a staff which
appeared to consist of the 'ah-me-I-was-a-pale-young-
curate-then' type. The *Daily Express* men were cocky
and confident. *The Times* staff were not pedantic or
ponderous but had the mellowed gaiety of a youngish
middle-aged Oxford don. The *Daily Mail* staff, on the
other hand, during the Northcliffe proprietorship,
reflected the mysterious air so beloved of the Chief
himself. Many tales could be told to illustrate this
point, but let this personal one suffice.

When the Italians bombarded Corfu, I was ordered
post-haste to Athens. I secured a lower berth on the
night train from the Gare de Lyon. I arrived early at
the station, saw my luggage placed in my berth and
then walked away to buy the evening newspapers. I
met the immaculate Mr G. Ward Price, Special
Correspondent of the *Daily Mail*. A shining monocle
in his eye, an impressively rolled umbrella, he might
have been about to stroll down Bond Street. 'Hullo',
he said. 'Where are you off to?'

'I am going to Athens', I said. 'Where are you going?'

'Oh, nowhere', he said airily. We wished one another good-night and I returned to my berth.

Now there was a mass of beautiful luggage in the upper berth. Idly I turned round a label to see the name of my travelling companion. It was G. Ward Price. He was going to Rome.

By no means all the *Daily Mail* staff wore this hall-mark of Northcliffian-inspired mystery; I would exempt, for example, Tom Webster, the former Birmingham station booking clerk who became the famous sporting cartoonist of the *Daily Mail*. By all accounts Webster must be the reincarnation of the legendary Phil May. Neither would I include the gay and debonair Ferdinand Tuohy, who had a meteoric career on the *Daily Mail*. In his autobiography Tuohy quotes freely from the famous Northcliffe daily bulletins. For instance: 'Watch Prohibition. These damned Yanks will be drying us up before we know where we are.' The 'damned Yanks' from the North-cliffe who headed the British wartime mission to the U.S.A. is curious, but on other occasions Northcliffe was heard to refer to the inhabitants of the U.S.A. as 'White Chinese'!

Tuohy was enlightening as regards Northcliffe's relations with his staff, full of kindness and generosity one minute and full of fire and brimstone the next; the journalist also showed, incidentally, how the Chief liked to 'play off' one man against the other, which, as Tuohy shrewdly remarked, 'must have contributed much to the general malaise Carmelite House suffered from at this stage'. (It is the immediate post-war No. 1 period which is now under review.)

Tuohy gave two instances of Northcliffe seizing a telephone and angrily calling his office and making it appear that he, Tuohy, had been tale-bearing. 'One

J

could have kicked Northcliffe there and then', said Tuohy. 'However, since kicking one's proprietor but seldom leads to concrete advancement, I refrained. . .'

Some little time later, Tuohy was sent to Constantinople, when he dispatched himself to the delightful island of Prinkipo in the Sea of Marmora and sent a story to the *Daily Mail* which gave rise to this passage in Northcliffe's daily bulletin: 'Why is Tuohy spending my money on Russian women in Turkey when he ought to be in Scotland writing about drink, a subject of which he should not, however, be allowed to get too full?' Tuohy allowed us to learn that very soon after this he departed from the *Daily Mail*.

Like many another young reporter who basked for a short while in the sunshine of the Chief's smile, Tuohy was invited to the Northcliffe home for lunch. Another member of the staff also once so invited records Northcliffe as exclaiming: 'It's only a simple luncheon, eggs, veal, grouse and tart', a delightfully naïve statement. Several of Northcliffe's biographers go to great pains to disclaim that wealth and honours meant anything to Northcliffe, but a little story of Ward Price's, concerning an incident which occurred one day while Northcliffe was in Paris, refutes the biographers' statements, I suggest.

Ward Price had written a letter to his Chief, addressing it: 'Lord Northcliffe . . .' When Ward Price met the Chief, Northcliffe took an envelope out of his pocket and said: 'Look here, Ward Price, I don't care, of course, how you write me, but here'— showing the envelope—'is how a Royal Princess wrote me yesterday.' The envelope was addressed: 'The Right Honourable the Lord Northcliffe . . .'

The malaise to which Tuohy referred must surely have arisen out of some of Northcliffe's extraordinary

eccentric rulings and their reactions on members of
his staff. Once he had two men, Philip Gibbs and
Filson Young, editing the same paper. A then prominent member of the staff said that these two men
were each claiming to sit in the chair of Editor-in-
Chief. As soon as one rose, the other seized the chair.
Victory went at last to the one who could for the
longest time resist the imperious calls of nature.
Northcliffe was most amused.

The newspaper with the twin editors was not the
Daily Mail; it is understood that it was the *Weekly
Dispatch*, which was once brilliantly edited during the
Northcliffe *régime* by Hannen Swaffer, who the Chief
nicknamed the 'Poet', supposedly because Swaffer
wore his hair somewhat longer than the orthodox
manner. Swaffer has become a legendary figure in
British journalism. 'Fired' by Northcliffe and then re-
installed after a period of adversity, Swaffer is the hero
of many Northcliffe yarns. It is said that once Northcliffe cabled Swaffer: 'Understand Pierre Loti rouges
his lips, paints his face Stop send good story'. To
which Swaffer is said to have cabled back: 'Regret
Pierre Loti refuses rouge lips paint face even for me'.

Swaffer was one of Northcliffe's 'No men', perhaps
at the time the only one. A fearless journalist who
'stood up' to Northcliffe and wrote the truth as he saw
it, Swaffer's second turn of duty with Northcliffe also
came to an end.

Thomas Marlowe who edited the *Daily Mail* for a
quarter of a century must also have been one of the
fearless breed. He was a power of strength to the paper
during its palmiest days, but he must have found the
going very difficult.

Tom Clarke, a keen observer, says that Mr Marlowe
was always fidgety when Northcliffe was about, and

that he put up with a lot of nagging. Clarke witnessed
scenes between them so painful that he wanted nothing
less than to 'fall through the floor to escape seeing any
more'. Towards the end, there was tension between
proprietor and editor, but Northcliffe could never
trust himself to let Marlowe go.

On February 22, 1922, Northcliffe cabled from the
South of France to the News Editor of the *Daily Mail*
demanding to know the meaning of the word 'ectoplasm' which had appeared in a leading article in the
newspaper. Northcliffe also demanded to be told the
name of the man who had written the article. Actually,
what had happened was that Mr Marlowe had himself
inserted the word 'ectoplasm' in the article. The
News Editor took Northcliffe's cable to Marlowe and
asked him what he should do about it. Marlowe
turned white when he read the message; he said to the
News Editor: 'You can say what the hell you like. I
don't give a damn what you say!'

Mr Hamilton Fyfe was working on the *Morning
Advertiser* when Northcliffe engaged him. Fyfe, it was
said, made it one of his conditions that his friend
George Curnock, working on the same newspaper,
should also join the *Daily Mail*. Northcliffe undoubtedly became very fond of Hamilton Fyfe and
gave him many choice assignments. When Fyfe left the
Daily Mail, and it would seem that most of these
thumbnail sketches finish with that phrase, his ideas
seemed to move far from Jingo Journalism, and we
read of him editing and writing in publications of
somewhat Left tendencies.

George Curnock became the director of the Northcliffe 'stunts'. It was Curnock who in 1914 launched
'Tipperary'; he found the B.E.F. singing that song
while encamped on the hills around Boulogne. His

story made the song, an unknown pantomime song of the previous winter. The song publishers must have reaped a huge fortune. Some years later I met Curnock in the London Press Club. We talked about 'Tipperary'. He took a silver cigarette case from his pocket and showed it to me. 'That's all I got out of it', he said bitterly.

J. M. Jeffries, more ambassadorial looking than most Ambassadors, was one of Northcliffe's bright young men. Jeffries, a staunch Roman Catholic, is an emotional writer of the greatest sincerity. On one occasion the story he was 'covering' for the *Daily Mail* led him into a *contretemps* because he felt so strongly; this happened in Athens, where another and more amusing adventure befell him. One fine sunny afternoon, Jeffries, having a few idle hours on his hands, went for a solitary walk in the country. He sat down on a hillside and thought he would sunbathe. He removed his clothes and fell asleep. A passing shepherd took a fancy to the journalist's kit. When he awoke, Jeffries was very uncovered and without the wherewithal to cover his nakedness. Two *gendarmes* found him in this condition, but Jeffries, equipped only with classical Greek, was unable to explain the circumstances. Finally the *gendarmes* found a piece of sacking, so, draping this around the Englishman, they took him in to Athens. I am as sure as if I had witnessed this scene that although Jeffries lost his clothes he never lost his ambassadorial poise.

As proof of Jeffries' sincerity and emotion, I may perhaps cite this story which redounds entirely to the credit of the journalist. Jeffries was assigned to 'cover' the burial of the Unknown Soldier. Suddenly, so it is said, as the afternoon wore on, the News Editor realised that Jeffries had not 'turned in' his story. Somebody

was told to telephone Jeffries' home. A maid replied
that Mr Jeffries was so overcome that he had taken to
his bed.

Yes, I am afraid the completed thumbnail sketch
of my good friend, J. M. Jeffries, must be rounded off
in the usual way. He left the *Daily Mail* at the height
of his powers, with a pension, and wrote a most
excellent book.

The late Walter Fish was for a long time News
Editor of the *Daily Mail*. Sometimes Northcliffe would
telephone Fish and solemnly ask: 'Anything fresh,
Fish?'

The late W. L. Warden, a stout little man, bounded
off the Gordon Bennett bat on to the Northcliffe
wicket. For long years he worked in Paris for the
American millionaire newspaper proprietor. Then
came the first World War. The Germans advanced on
Paris and Warden beat a strategic retreat to London.
He called at the London office of the *New York Herald*,
where the knowledge of his retreat had preceded him.
'Mr Warden to see you, sir', announced the office
boy to John Burke, the London correspondent of the
Herald. The boy left the door open behind him.
'Throw the man out!' roared Burke. 'He must be an
impostor! Warden is at his post in Paris, a post of
danger! He is defying the Germans, so throw that
impostor out!'

But Warden had the last laugh. He joined Northcliffe's staff and returned to Paris when all danger had
passed and became Editor of the *Continental Daily
Mail*.

Northcliffe liked to keep his men on tenterhooks
and would often enough ring them in the early hours
of the morning, pretending to be surprised they were
still in bed. Another trick of his was to call a man into

his room, tell him to go to the far corner of the room, then the Chief would put his hands over his mouth and speak softly. If the unfortunate fellow could not hear, Northcliffe would exclaim petulantly: 'As I thought, deaf as a post. Go to my Harley Street specialist and get your ears examined.'

With Warden, Northcliffe used a particularly refined form of persecution. He often took this employee travelling with him. When he heard Warden splashing in his bath, he would have him summoned to his presence. The fat little fellow would come bouncing in, in his dressing-gown. 'Ah, Warden, there you are, eh?' exclaimed the Chief. 'That's all right, then.'

One one occasion, when some poor devil had incurred Northcliffe's displeasure, he had him summoned to Paris. Northcliffe for the occasion had a suite of which one room had many doors, like in one of the old-time Palais Royal farces. The victim was placed in this room, then secretaries kept on rushing in through unexpected doors, telling the victim the dire things Northcliffe was going to do to him. Northcliffe, however, had his moments of gentleness, particularly before the mental malady had become his master. Then, sometimes, he would, after giving a man a bad 'dressing down', send him a message telling him not to worry too much.

It was in France, at Versailles, that we come across another perplexing twist to the strange character of Northcliffe. It was the secretary concerned in this matter who told me the story.

This secretary had a curious Chinese puzzle made of wood. One day he left it on the mantelpiece of his room in a Versailles hotel where he was accompanying his Chief. When the secretary returned to his room from some errand he found that someone had dismantled the puzzle. The secretary mentioned the matter casually to Northcliffe. The Chief sent for the *maître d'hôtel*, one Joseph, a German, and said to him: 'I have here a Chinese ornament which I have had for a long time; somebody has dismantled it. It must be put together again, without fail, before tomorrow morning.'

'Very good, my lord', said the *maître d'hôtel*, bowing himself out, with the puzzle. All that night the staff sat up trying to solve the puzzle, without success. At breakfast time a pale-faced Joseph entered the presence with the still-dismantled puzzle in his hand. 'I regret, my lord', said Joseph, 'that we cannot put this together again.'

'Come, come', said Northcliffe, 'that won't do, you know. You take that thing over there to the window and put it together yourself and I will give you £100.'

For two hours Joseph struggled; then in a fury, the German threw the puzzle on the floor, shouting: 'I can't do it', and went out of the room.

'That will teach the servants not to touch things that don't concern them', was Northcliffe's comment.

The same secretary tells another Northcliffe story. He was with the Chief on a golfing holiday near Wimereux. Every day the secretary had to go to Boulogne to meet the Folkestone boat which brought the London newspapers. These he took to the golf course to meet Northcliffe. 'Come on, come on! What does the *Daily Express* say?' Northcliffe would shout, taking a swipe at the ball. Down on his knees dropped the secretary, opening the desired paper and trying to prevent the Channel breezes blowing away the sheets. By this time Northcliffe, having caught up with the ball, would shout: 'Come on, come *on*! What does *The Times* say?' Again the secretary knelt among the newspapers, searching and finding and gathering together the wind-swept newspapers, only to find that the Chief was in a bunker, but perhaps not so bunkered as his perspiring secretary.

Frank Harris, who had a caustic wit, always referred to Perrier water as 'Harmsworth juice', a *boutade* built on the fact that this famous table water belonged to one of Northcliffe's brothers, St John Harmsworth. The story of how Perrier became a Harmsworth property is an example of the 'Harmsworth luck', and should, I think, find a place here. The story was told me by the late Walter Crotch, founder of the Dickens Fellowship.

'Some years ago', said Mr Crotch, 'I accompanied a party of British and French engineers on a trip to the Gard to verify the reported discovery of a mispickel mine alleged to be of great value. It was located in the vicinity of Arles, which lay at the foot of the mountain upon which the mine was supposed to exist. Emerging from our rather primitive hotel in the morning, I noticed that a stream of most beautifully clear but petillant water was running down the open gutters of streets. "It looks fit to drink!" I ejaculated. "It is", replied the hotel proprietor. "I have plenty inside; taste it." I did. It was clean to the palate, cool and refreshing. "What makes it sparkle and bubble?" I asked. "It is entirely natural sparkling water", I was told. It made an impression on my mind but that was all.'

'Years afterwards I had occasion to motor to Nimes and a whim took me the fifty or less kilometres to the district of the phantom mispickel mine, but the sparkling water had disappeared; at least, it no longer flowed in abandonment down the streets, a free gift of Nature to the inhabitants of the region. I enquired what had become of it, and was told that an Englishman had passed that way and had been impressed with that clear limpid water, just as I had been years before. But he had done something more than dream about it. He had motored up to the source and promptly proceeded to acquire all the uplands, including the spring, had formed a company and was now bottling the water and was selling it under the name of "Perrier". I asked the name of the Englishman. It was unpronounceable, save that it was Singeon Something. I discovered that it was that of St John Harmsworth, Lord Northcliffe's younger brother.'

Frank Harris, to whom Northcliffe was allergic, had a theory that Northcliffe was not a great man, because he did not know how to choose his lieutenants. Harris's theory is not sustained by factual evidence; rather would it seem that in some cases his choice was imperfect in design. Like many men in similar situations, Northcliffe was surrounded at different times by a chorus of 'yes-men'. On the other hand, a number of men who found that Northcliffe's methods and manners were opposed to their conscience, preferred to part from him. A striking case in point was that of the late Valentine Williams.

Williams, who had served Northcliffe well as Foreign Correspondent, was appointed Foreign Editor. While occupying this post he began to write books which achieved success. Northcliffe objected to Williams writing books. Williams, after much heart-searching, resigned—and became an outstanding 'best-seller'.

Williams introduced Rothsay Reynolds to Northcliffe. Northcliffe appointed Reynolds *Daily Mail* Berlin correspondent. After Reynolds had withdrawn from the first meeting, Northcliffe said to Williams:

'Tell your friend that I like his face'. Perhaps this was as good a reason as any to appoint a correspondent in Berlin, although a curious one, but Reynolds, who died during the war, was a curious person himself.

Reynolds had been the British Embassy Chaplain in St Petersburg. He was converted to Roman Catholicism, became a journalist, and, eventually, a strong supporter of Fascism, but this was after Northcliffe's death. During their joint life-time he was an outstanding yes-man.

A predecessor of Reynolds in Berlin was a German-American named Wilhelm Friedrich Weil, who, when he was naturalised British, anglicised his name to William Frederick Wile. In July 1919, Northcliffe told me that 'Wile was the best spy England had in Germany', a statement to which much doubt may be attached. It was during this same conversation that Northcliffe informed me that 'Jews, Japs and Germans should all be treated alike'. He invited my agreement. When I demurred, he backed his argument with this statement: 'On the outbreak of war I had one of the most prominent Jews in London on his knees to me in *The Times* office, begging me to use my influence to prevent the war!'

What truth should be attached to this Northcliffian allegation? At the time he made it, the mental malady had probably reached the megalomaniac stage. Moreover, Northcliffe was primed with bitterness; he had not been allowed to become a member of the British Peace Delegation to Paris; he had seen his hopes of the Premiership of Britain thrust on one side, but I would suggest that his always-present dislike of the Jews—to put it no higher than that—accounted for his outburst. To this 'Jew-baiting' habit of Northcliffe I have already referred, but it is worthy of greater attention, because it was a cross-section of his mind, and for those who would form an unbiased judgement of his character, it is of importance.

Mr O. J. Pulvermacher, who, although a son of a well-to-do Jewish family, began his career on the *Daily Mail* in a very junior capacity, working his way to a high level, told me that once and once only did Northcliffe ever make a reference to his race, and that was when he referred to him as 'Oriental Pulvermacher'. On the other hand, another Jew, Bernard Falk, who worked so long with Harmsworth, Northcliffe and Rothermere (the first Lord Rothermere), writes much of Northcliffe's unkind 'cracks' at himself as a Jew and at the Jewish race in general. Falk must be a most even-tempered man, and, of course, he had his own job to protect. Only once, apparently, did he ever come near to losing his temper. That was when, after enduring Northcliffe 'Jew-baiting' while he was the newspaper proprietor's luncheon guest, he burst out: 'Let's talk about the Scots for a change, Chief'. Falk was on a good wicket there, because Northcliffe's dislike of the Scots was second only to his dislike of the Jews.

Northcliffe was a generous entertainer of his staff, sometimes in bulk and sometimes in small groups, but one wonders whether some of them did not mentally echo the wish of Ferdinand Tuohy, who, as stated, felt that he could kick his proprietor. Northcliffe often gilded the lily when he invited members of his staff to stay with him on the Riviera or at Pau, which he carefully pointed out must be pronounced 'Po', but when they were his guests we find him acting not so much like a rich uncle, as a *nouveau-riche* uncle. We find him, for instance, at Menton, asking his guests: 'Did the financial pundits in London fix you boys up all right? I ordered them to book you by the Riviera Express, the finest and most luxurious train in the world, and to advance £50 each and no questions asked.' This might have proved as fairy-uncle-ish as it sounds, but experience proved that the guests had a rough passage when they tried to cash in on the Chief's promise.

We find him asking Tom Clarke: 'Did you lose money at the Casino last night? . . . I will instruct my secretary to let you young men have some money every night—100 francs or so—(approximately £2 10s. at this time: 1921) to spend at the tables.' On the same visit, to an editor: 'Take these young men and buy them the most expensive lunch you can buy, and it has not to cost them a penny. I want them to see what a really expensive lunch is like.' It must be added that his guests were all married householders, occupying posts of editorial responsibility on Northcliffe's publications.

A dinner party given by Northcliffe shortly after he purchased *The Times* had a somewhat curious sequel; in fact, the story must end on a note of interrogation. There was a member of the staff of *The Times* named Crippen to whom Northcliffe became extremely attached; he took him everywhere with him, and it was arranged that at this dinner party Crippen was to make a speech. Evidently Northcliffe believed that the speech would show the beneficial influence his publications, such as the *Daily Mail*, would have on *The Times*. Crippen made his speech, but the trend of the discourse was to show the beneficial influence *The Times* would have on the *Daily Mail*. Northcliffe, who had no sense of humour when there was any question of the *Daily Mail*, and far be it from me to suggest that the Crippen speech had any humorous intent, was

livid with anger. *Crippen disappeared!* Where he went,
how he went or what became of him, nobody knows.
One of Northcliffe's secretaries, who was in daily
contact with the Chief at that time, tells me that all he
knows is that Crippen vanished. Was his fare paid to
some distant colony? Nobody knew.

In June 1921, a Welsh choir visited London to
raise money for miners' families hit by the coal strike.
The choir was singing outside Carmelite House when
Northcliffe came through on the telephone to Tom
Clarke. The Chief could hear the singing faintly; he
asked what it was and when informed, told Clarke to
give the miners £5 from the *Daily Mail*. 'Let it be given
publicly', he ordered, 'to let the crowd see how
generous we are.'

This was done. Clarke gave the money to Glover,
the commissionaire, who told Clarke he had been
given orders to stop the miners entering Carmelite
House to collect money!

Glover, incidentally, was quite a character. He had
been a member of the London police force and spoke
fluent French. At a moment when Northcliffe's actions
were becoming most unpredictable, to say the least,
he made Glover controller of advertisements in the
Daily Mail, with orders to throw out the advertisements he did not like!

After Northcliffe's death, a large portrait of him
was hanging in the vestibule of Northcliffe House.
Glover, who continued as commissionaire, said to one
of Northcliffe's former secretaries, nodding towards the
portrait: 'D'you know, sir, he *speaks* to me!'

I have endeavoured to show that despite such actions
as the Glover appointment, Northcliffe was just as
much interested in securing advertisements—and
rightly so—as other newspaper proprietors, but one

may perhaps mention one more advertising story which shows that even in relations with his editors, Northcliffe liked occasionally to pose as the detached person to whom advertising was really a bit of a bore.

When Bernard Falk was editing Northcliffe's *Weekly Dispatch*, the Chief telephoned him to 'hide' the advertisements when he considered he had too many. I wonder what would have happened to him if he had followed his Chief's advice?

Perhaps the apotheosis of Northcliffe's relations with the *Daily Mail* was reached on the occasion of the banquet he gave to the whole staff at Olympia, London, in May, 1921, to celebrate the twenty-fifth birthday of the paper. A clergyman was engaged to say Grace and recite a special prayer for 'Thy servant Alfred'.

The high moment came when Northcliffe, with his mother, not Lady Northcliffe, on his arm, perambulated the hall to receive the plaudits of the staff.

The banquet was arranged for a Sunday. The staff was pressed to attend the meal. Olympia was crowded, but nevertheless there were some vacant places; the Chief was furious. Directly the lunch was over, Northcliffe had himself driven to Carmelite House personally to superintend the setting up of the story of his feast in the paper. A skeleton staff was on duty until the return of the others from Olympia. Northcliffe, in the bullying blustering way with which he so often domineered his employees, ordered that a shorthand writer should be brought to him immediately. The man who came was shivering with fright, poor wretch, and was unable to take the notes shouted at him. Northcliffe became more furious; he thundered that the man was drunk and that he had drunk too much at the banquet. Not only was the man not drunk, but he was a member of the skeleton staff and, as such, had not attended the Olympia festivities. Notwithstanding, the Chief used his inevitable weapon: he told the News Editor the man was to be 'sacked'!

The News Editor protested by letter, saying that this reporter had given long and valuable service to the paper, and, in any case, he was not a professional shorthand writer. Northcliffe wrote another letter upholding his decision, but later telephoned to say that 'the matter had been fixed up satisfactorily'.

After the war, Northcliffe, to everyone's surprise, made Campbell Stuart Managing Editor of the *Daily Mail* despite that he had no newspaper experience whatever. Later Campbell Stuart was made Manager of *The Times*. When Northcliffe died, there were sweeping changes and, as a partial result, the young Canadian was able to devote his activities to other endeavours, given a title and achieved considerable wealth; another example of the heights to which talented men on the 'business side' of Northcliffe's publications could climb.

Writing of Sir Campbell Stuart, Mr Hamilton Fyfe stresses this phrase of Northcliffe's life in relation to Campbell Stuart as follows: 'Never until now had he (Northcliffe) been able to endure for any length of time a personal assistant whom he had to treat as his social equal. He preferred to have about him . . . persons of a social standing lower than his own. . . . Now at last one succeeded.'

Campbell Stuart possibly had very wide powers within the Northcliffe framework, but on one occasion the Chief exercised his veto. When Stuart Campbell was with *The Times* he needed a secretary. A young man recently out of the Army applied for the post. Campbell sent him to Northcliffe to be 'vetted'.

'Well, young man', said the Chief, 'how much is *The Times* paying for ink?'

The young man did not know. How could he? He did not get the post.

I should add that the young man is now known to fame as Vernon Bartlett.

In concluding this record of Northcliffe and some of the members of the staff, I would like to tell a little story told me by Mr Basil Cardew, son of Mr Roger Cardew who worked thirty-eight years on the *Daily Mail* and was killed in a road accident while on duty.

'When the *Daily Mail* held a week's celebrations to mark its fiftieth birthday', Mr Cardew told me, 'I expected my mother to be invited to one of the ceremonies or banquets. As no invitation to my mother was forthcoming, I racked my brains how best to jolt the memories of the *Daily Mail* executives. On Friday, May 10, 1946—a year and five days after my father's death—the idea came to me while riding on top of a 'bus that stopped beside St Dunstan's-in-the-West, Fleet Street. The bust of Lord Northcliffe gave me the idea and I at once wrote a letter to *The Times* which was published the next day.'

Here is the letter:

The Editor, *The Times*.
Sir,

As one who was literally brought up with the *Daily Mail*—my late father served them faithfully for thirty-eight years—I should have thought the happy celebrations of last week marking the fiftieth birthday of this newspaper would have included the placing of some token of appreciation at the foot of the bust of Lord Northcliffe, in the courtyard of St Dunstan's-in-

K

the-West, Fleet Street, which was recently uncovered after being bricked up during the war years.

Yours etc.

BASIL CARDEW.

NORTHCLIFFE'S Napoleonic complex, if one admits it existed, provides yet another interesting sidelight on his character. There is evidence that Northcliffe was one of those people who would liked to have played the leading part on a stage well bathed in limelight, and, at the same time, to sit in the stalls applauding himself. Some of Northcliffe's biographers refuse to admit there was any disposition to what is commonly called swollen-headedness, but the evidence speaks for itself. He was blatant, but he could pour out charm when so he willed; he was blustering, but he could be gentle. Were not these traits also attributed to Napoleon Bonaparte?

Should we accept the premises that Northcliffe did indeed possess a Napoleonic complex, or not? Sir Max Pemberton affirmed that the story is all nonsense, that it was merely a whimsical invention of the late E. V. Lucas. We must not forget that Pemberton knew Northcliffe intimately for many years, and was in close touch with him both professionally and socially. We must listen to what others have to say about this Napoleonic complex which in the opinion of some amounted to Northcliffe's belief that he was the reincarnation of Napoleon Bonaparte.

First of all let us go way back and hear Julian

Ralph, a war correspondent in the Boer War, who said to the late R. D. Blumenfeld, 'I have been talking to young Alfred Harmsworth, a most remarkable personality who is bound to do big things, if for no other reason that he probably believes that he is Napoleon come back to life. The next time you talk to him, try and remember this and see if you cannot pick out the little Napoleonic gestures and peculiarities.'

Blumenfeld added some enlightening comment of his own. 'It was impossible for me to dissociate him from Napoleon', said Blumenfeld. 'He accentuated the wisp of hair over his forehead, he gesticulated just as Marshal Bertrand described Napoleon's gesticulations; he barked out quick commands to sub-editors and chauffeurs alike, just as no doubt the Little Corsican barked to his Marshals and his Guard sergeants. I noticed a distinct preference for busts of Napoleon which you could see in almost any room that Harmsworth occupied. Finally, as the years passed on and he became a peer, he sent me one day a note signed "N" which was, of course, the Napoleonic cipher. The regal-looking "N" completed the illusion.'

'I was mischievous enough once in chatting with him to say that I presumed he had chosen Northcliffe for his titular name in preference to the obvious and more widely known Harmsworth, merely to be able to use the Napoleonic "N" in future correspondence. Knowing his predilection for publicity in all its phases —though at first he sought none personally—I could only attribute his choice to the greater claim on his imagination. He had a sense of humour which was generally under control. He did not check it this time, for he laughed and said: "No, you are wrong. I wanted very much to call myself Lord Harmsworth—

not as you would suggest, for the purpose of advertising my publications, but simply on account of a
pardonable family pride. The authorities who distil
red blood into blue blood in the Privy Council or the
Lord Chamberlain's office or wherever they do their
distilling, would not permit me to use the name of
Harmsworth, for the reason which you mention—
advertising—and so I had to fall back on the usual
territorial descriptive title. . . ." '

Blumenfeld, no doubt, was 'pulling the Chief's leg',
for practically all the newspaper world knew that
Harmsworth took his title from the Thanet village so
close to his home at Elmwood, but is it not possible
that Northcliffe did like having a place name which
began with an 'N'? In a matter of choice of titles, and
one supposes such a choice existed, is it not extremely
probable that the Chief did indeed have a predilection
for a place with such an initial letter? Incidentally,
the cover of Mr McNair Wilson's life of Northcliffe is
decorated with the Napoleonic cipher, and as for the
letter signed with a regal 'N' which Blumenfeld says
he received, very many other people received such
letters, and, indeed, when the megalomanic phase
was in the full period, you will find Northcliffe's
notepaper was headed with the regal and Napoleonic
cipher 'N'.

Blumenfeld also records another likeness between
Northcliffe and Napoleon Bonaparte. 'People who
knew Napoleon Bonaparte well always said that one of
his marked characteristics was of lolling luxuriously
in an armchair. He would fling himself almost with
violence into a large chair and at once assume an air
of ease and comfort unexpectedly different from the
exhibition of fierce activity which he had displayed
only a few seconds before.

'That, too, was one of the characteristics of the late Viscount Northcliffe. Whenever I think of him I have in my mind the picture of a corpulent loosely dressed man, humped up purringly in an armchair. You could even tell his moods from the manner in which he rolled himself up or stretched himself out. If he was pleased, he lay as prone and flat as the chair would permit; if he was arguing, he sat up as if he was ready to spring, which he frequently did.'

One direct reference to Napoleon made by Northcliffe is recorded by Blumenfeld. It happened during a conversation at Crewe House, during the seven months period when Northcliffe was Director of Propaganda against Enemy Countries, but before recalling his actual words, this is how he described Northcliffe at this period, at the end of 1917, through the eyes of a trained and brilliant observer.

'I had not seen him for many months', wrote Blumenfeld. 'The change in the man was too great to be unnoticed. There was a look about him which showed the effects of adulation in America, the never-ceasing floods of flattery, the stories of how he had forced Asquith out and Lloyd George in, the David who had defeated the Goliath Kitchener in the shell-shortage scandal; and the thousand and one pleasant-hearing tales of his public courage, his incorruptibility, his sense of duty and his complete sacrifice to the war spirit—all had been ladled out to him with the inevitable affect of causing him to believe that it was all true and that he was the sole instrument appointed to bring glory to his country and its cause.' Now for the Napoleonic reference. 'Do you remember', Northcliffe asked Blumenfeld, 'how Napoleon always relied on propaganda as much as battalions to disrupt his enemies?'

But one can go even further back than that for the purpose of tracing the alleged likeness between North-cliffe and Napoleon; there was a similarly real or imagined likeness between the mothers of the two men.

Mr Hamilton Fyfe, writing of the *Answers* period, said: 'He has now a Napoleonic belief in his destiny. Frequently he is told of his likeness to Napoleon. He is pleased by this. He begins to collect portraits and small possessions of the Emperor. He starts a Napoleonic cult. Later he will sign himself with a single initial which is not unlike the imperial "N".'

'He is, in truth, far more handsome than the young Bonaparte ever was, even in the eyes of that adoring yet critical parent Leticia. (Northcliffe: "Curious that I should have a mother critical and adoring, too".')

I never had an opportunity of asking Sir Max Pemberton to comment on that, because during the last years of his life he was very ill, but it is difficult for me to explain away his airy dismissal of the Napoleonic legend, if legend it was, and blame it all on to E. V. Lucas.

Mr Tom Clarke has a story which gives light on the Napoleon complex from another angle. Clarke said that in 1921 he picked up a copy of the *Occult Review* containing Northcliffe's horoscope. He spoke to Northcliffe about it; Northcliffe appeared to be surprised, but Clarke says he fancies that Northcliffe inspired this attempt to read the starring indication of his fate and fortune on the eve of the start of the world tour.

The Chief kept up his real or feigned surprise during the opening sentences of his subsequent conversation with Clarke. Northcliffe said it was not possible for the publication to have his horoscope, because they would not know at what time of day he was born.

Clarke, reading from the article, quoted four in the afternoon as the given time. Northcliffe replied that this was 'about right' because his mother had told him that his father, who was in the garden, threw his cap in the air when they came and told him his first-born was a son. Northcliffe, curiously enough, did not ask Clarke to show him a copy of the *Occult Review* he had with him, but said he 'must see it', because he was very superstitious. There was further talk, and then Clarke, again reading from the horoscope, quoted it as stating that Northcliffe would always have to take care of his health. To that, Northcliffe replied that he had been ill very often, but it did not worry him; he had, so he said, spent three years of his life in bed with various illnesses. He then switched the conversation back to the *Occult Review* and told Clarke to procure him sixty copies of the paper because he wanted to send them to various people.

Now the point of this story is that the horoscope was built around the legend of the two 'N's'—Napoleon and Northcliffe. If one subtracts the usual vague padding one finds in most horoscopes, the concrete part of the Northcliffe horoscope rests on various allusions to 'curious coincidences' such as the perhaps unimportant fact that the centenary of Napoleon's death occurred just one day earlier than the twenty-fifth anniversary of the foundation of the *Daily Mail*. On firmer ground perhaps is the horoscope when it explains that both Napoleon and Northcliffe were born beneath the same sign of the Zodiac and that both began life with little prospect of success, both were members of large families and both found the means to raise their brothers to affluence and power.

As regards general influence, the horoscope cast the statement that Northcliffe would not feel the full beneficial influences until he reached early middle life (he was, however, fifty-six when the horoscope was published). Death, it was said, might come suddenly. It came, not by any means suddenly, a year and four months after the horoscope was published.

Did Northcliffe really inspire the casting and publication of his horoscope, as Mr Tom Clarke suggests? One supposes that the suspicion, whether justified or not, is mainly based on the Napoleonic allusions, but if one accepts the thesis that this alleged resemblance between the First Consul of France and the founder of the *Daily Mail* was generally known in journalistic circles, where it was usually treated as either a harmless fallacy or a freak of fate, according to the mentality of the person discussing the matter, it is equally possible that Northcliffe was entirely guiltless of having inspired the article, but it by no means acquits him of believing that he was the re-incarnation of Napoleon Bonaparte, or else there was some very close affinity between himself and the Little Corsican. So far, the evidence consists of one life-long friend, Sir Max Pemberton, dismissing the story; several people who were in close contact with North-cliffe and who believe the opposite; and two direct Northcliffe quotations drawing comparisons between his own mother and Napoleon's and comparing his propaganda with Napoleon's. Another direct piece of evidence is also supplied by Mr Tom Clarke, who passed through Fontainebleau with the Chief in the beginning of April 1922. Clarke tells how he was packed off to see the Napoleon relics in the Palace, with Northcliffe's order: 'And you must see them all. Go and see the wonderful things in the kitchen. I will send over to the chief guide and see you tip him well. There are lots of places they do not show to ordinary visitors.' When Clarke returned, Northcliffe closely questioned him as to what he had seen; he mentioned things Clarke apparently had not seen. Northcliffe was dissatisfied. 'You did not pay the guide well enough. Go back and tell him I have sent you. You must see the other things, and pay him well. . . . You'll find Napoleon's hat there. I once had it on. *It fits me!*'

SOME day somebody will, I hope, write the story of Olympia, London; it is one of London's landmarks; it was the scene of several successes of my old friend the late Sir Charles B. Cochran, Britain's leading showman, who was, in his own field, just as great a conqueror as the hero of this biographical study was in his. Cochran and Northcliffe knew one another. Cochran the showman, who, like all showmen, depended largely on the good-will of the Press, probably knew some time previous to January 1912 that, if need be, Northcliffe would help him out of a difficulty, but it is unlikely that Cochran in his wildest dreams could ever have seen himself such a lavished pet of the Press as Northcliffe made him during a brief but hectic interlude in the *Daily Mail.*

Olympia has been many things to many people. It was once the 'big top' of Barnum and Bailey's Circus when it made its first appearance in the British Isles; it was the first time London had seen a three-ringed circus. Olympia became the setting for prize-fights, for the vain seeking out of a British 'White Hope' to win the heavyweight crown of laurels, but Olympia must on this occasion be regarded as the particular background for the changing London into which Alfred Harmsworth projected his *Daily Mail,* for Olympia in many ways was the mirror which reflected the possibilities for a more colourful life for the masses, a thing that Alfred Harmsworth helped to bring about by way of presenting dramatised news. Behold then, Olympia, when three brothers named Kiralfy came to Kensington from the Balkans, via the U.S.A. Imré Kiralfy had been with Barnum's in the States. Where they obtained their financial backing, I do not know, but in Olympia one dank winter they produced a show called 'Venice'. Gondolas in darkest Kensington! Real honest-to-God gondoliers singing on a replica of the Grand Canal! Here was romance, here was glamour, but in those days England had never used the word, with or without the 'u'! For a humble 'tanner' one could go to 'Venice', but rides on the Canal were, of course, extra.

When London goes to a show it wants to eat and to drink. This great truism occurred to a young man named Joseph Lyons, who obtained the catering contract for Olympia and installed a monster kitchen beneath the stage. Harmsworth was getting on, but he was not blazing a lone trail. Others were likewise bent towards self-help and progress. 'Venice in Kensington' was Joe Lyons' first step to success; he fixed his headquarters in nearby Cadby Hall, where they remained. The Kiralfys did what it is very difficult to do: they repeated a success. 'Venice' truimphed a second winter in London.

For the third winter the Kiralfys put on another successful water show: 'Constantinople'. Then they went and Kensington returned to inner and outer darkness.

We must now move forward with the years and come to 1911 when, after Olympia had been the setting for many shows and exhibitions, Mr Cochran decided that London must see something startlingly

novel. He had hied himself to Berlin where he entered
into conferences with Max Reinhardt, of whom the
world was beginning to hear. After much coming and
going here and there, to Berlin and back again, to
Budapest and back again, Cochran decided he would
turn Olympia into a replica of a cathedral. Dr Karl
Vollmöller supplied the scenario, Humperdinck the
music, and Reinhardt did the production of *The
Miracle*, which was the Legend of Provence, the life of
a nun who goes out into the world. Cologne Cathedral
was the source of inspiration for the setting of the
Olympia 'cathedral'. The production of *The Miracle*
was financed by the company controlling Olympia;
profits were to be divided between Cochran and Mr
F. H. Payne, the Managing Director of Olympia.

The Miracle was produced on Christmas Eve, 1911;
very soon it was evident that there would be no profits.

Not that *The Miracle* was badly received; on the
contrary. But the audiences were not large enough.
The weekly salary list was in the neighbourhood of
£5,000, but then there were 1,500 people in the show!
'We had, perhaps, ten thousand people a day', said
Cochran, 'but we needed twenty thousand.'

Enter then Mr W. T. Stead, the eminent writing
crusader (later to be drowned in the *Titanic*). Stead
said to Cochran something that sounds curious. 'I can
praise it', he said, 'or I can attack it.' Stead proposed
writing two letters and sending them to Cochran for
the showman to make his pick. One letter was
criticism. The second letter, dated only three days
after the production, was, I think, a masterpiece. I
will quote part of it: 'I have just witnessed *The Miracle*.
But the miracle that impressed me most was the fact
that in this Protestant land you were not mobbed . . .
Think, sir, of the effect of this twice-a-day representa-

tion of Catholic ritual to eight thousand subjects of
our Protestant King, by the hired aid of another two
thousand men and women of this Protestant realm . . .
who present in the most attractive fashion the aes-
thetic lures of the Scarlet Woman. . . .'

'How much, sir, do you receive from the secret
service money of the Vatican or from the coffers of the
Jesuits for this imposing and magnificent propaganda
in favour of the Roman Catholic Church? . . .'

Cochran, being the great showman he was, accepted
the second letter, no doubt with his tongue in his
cheek. This letter was not sent by W. T. Stead to the
London newspapers belonging to the group then
known as the Northcliffe Press. I do not suggest that,
all things being the same, the Northcliffe papers would
not have published the Stead letter, but the fact of the
matter was that at this time W. T. Stead was barred
from being mentioned in the Northcliffe newspapers,
by order of Lord Northcliffe.

To the present generation the name of W. T. Stead
probably conveys very little, but in the late nineteenth
century and in the early twentieth he was one of the
giants among writing men. His name was constantly
before the public eye; his followers were legion, even
if his detractors were also fairly numerous, but it is
strange and somewhat grim to know that the pen of
such a master was at the pleasure of a showman, even
such a master showman as Cochran. Of course, one
does not blame Cochran in the very least; he being in
the show business had every right to take the utmost
advantage of any one who desired to break a lance on
his behalf. In any case, the Stead intervention did not
make up the difference between profit and loss. Then,
a little later, Northcliffe came on the scene.

Hamilton Fyfe, of the *Daily Mail* at the time, had

attended several rehearsals of *The Miracle*. It is more
than likely that Fyfe, a spiritual—albeit a somewhat
moody—person, was moved by the beauty of the
spectacle. Mr Wile, the Berlin correspondent of the
Daily Mail, attended the first performance of *The
Miracle* and was enthusiastic. Later Lady Northcliffe
came with her mother-in-law, Mrs Harmsworth. Lady
Northcliffe came again, with a member of the *Daily
Mail* staff, Mr Beach Thomas, later knighted. Lady
Northcliffe expressed her surprise to see the house
half empty. She told Cochran that she would bring
her husband when he returned to London.

Lord Northcliffe dropped in to see an afternoon
performance of *The Miracle*. Soon after he left Olympia
Cochran received a telephoned message from Mr
Hamilton Fyfe to say that the Northcliffe Press was
going to 'boom' *The Miracle*. The next morning the
Daily Mail came out with a letter signed by Mr
Hamilton Fyfe.

The letter showed surprise that *The Miracle* was
playing to such poor houses, but according to Cochran,
Mr Fyfe's letter made the receipts worse than they had
been. Whether Northcliffe had any definite plan in
his mind, may be regarded with some doubt. It is a
fact, however, recorded by Cochran himself, that the
letter was damaging to the show and, as he said at the
time, he would have rather the *Daily Mail* had let it
alone.

The day after the letter appeared, a representative
of the *Daily Mail* called on Cochran and asked to be
shown the returns for the matinee and evening per-
formances of *The Miracle* on *the day preceding the publication of Mr Hamilton Fyfe's letter*. Cochran admitted that
he faked the figures he gave. Actually business had
worsened; Cochran believed that the letter had caused

poorer business, but instead of giving a reply to this effect, the showman made out that business was better on account of the *Daily Mail* letter. Northcliffe fell for this deception; the next day the *Daily Mail* and other newspapers of the group cock-a-hooped that it had caused better business.

Northcliffe gave instructions to Hamilton Fyfe to write a story a day about *The Miracle*; other writers were put on to the story; every day the *Daily Mail* boosted the play. Business began to boom. The takings rose from £5,000 a week to £13,000 a week. There was never any suggestion that Northcliffe benefited directly or indirectly in any financial manner. Indeed, he gave instructions that Cochran was not to be allowed to increase his paid advertising, but Northcliffe benefited in prestige, his prestige as a 'stunt artist'. The man who made England eat Standard Bread and grow sweet peas, made people go to see a theatrical performance. The art of mass suggestion with its attendant dangers had triumphed again.

Lord Northcliffe possibly planned some sort of campaign, but it is not clear to me whether the campaign would have succeeded if Cochran had not taken the course he did. If he told the truth and said that as a result of Mr Fyfe's letter in the *Daily Mail* business had fallen off, what course could Northcliffe have steered? There is little evidence, I submit, of any wisdom or judgement—or genius—in this making of *The Miracle*. In figures the only difference the North-cliffe campaign made was that the show closed with a small profit instead of a loss. Yet the greatest irony was the pendant to the campaign; *The Miracle* could have made a really good profit if it could have had a longer run, but the show had to close because the *Daily Mail* Ideal Home Exhibition was due to open

Lord Northcliffe with his nephew, the present Lord Rothermere, next to him; on the extreme right is Harold, the first Lord Rothermere

Lord Northcliffe with his brother, the first Lord Rothermere

there! The man of whom it was said that it was he who had made *The Miracle* because of 'his appreciation of a rare and wondrous spectacle' could have made, if he wished, the great gesture of either postponing the Exhibition or moving it elsewhere; but he did no such thing. The 'stunt' was over; why worry? Yet I am not sure that Sir Charles Cochran was not a bigger worker of miracles than Lord Northcliffe

One knows how difficult it is for an artist to repeat a success with 'the mixture as before'. Mediocre comedians try and provoke laughs with the same gags and 'business', then become annoyed that audiences withhold their applause. Popular playwrights and actors sometimes try to produce sequels, pendants to their previous successes, and live to regret it.

In March 1922, Cochran produced an adaption of a French play called *L'Homme en Habit* at the Garrick Theatre, London. The English title was *The Man in Dress Clothes*. Seymour Hicks did the adaptation and played the leading part. 'For some weeks', wrote Cochran, 'the play ran to receipts of from £1,100 to as high as £1,600. Then the takings fell back to £1,300.'

Cochran makes the cryptic statement that Lord Northcliffe came a second time to the help of an enterprise with which he was associated; this time it was not because of his association, but 'rather in spite of it'.

Sir Max Pemberton went to see his old friend Northcliffe who had just returned to London from a trip abroad. In course of conversation, Pemberton told Northcliffe that Hicks was in a play that was not doing well. Northcliffe promised to see the play and attended an afternoon performance. He was given a box. Northcliffe saw Hicks during the second interval; he said he did not understand the play; he saw the last

L

act sitting on a chair in the wings. At the end of the performance, Northcliffe told Hicks that another notice of the play would appear in each of his newspapers. Hicks, possibly seeing a chance of obtaining more publicity, thanked Northcliffe, but said that his manager (Cochran) did not believe in the power of the Press. Northcliffe was immediately and not unnaturally nettled. 'Who is your manager?' asked Northcliffe. Hicks told him. 'Very well', said Northcliffe, 'I'll show him.'

According to Cochran, Northcliffe this time did not turn the boosting of the play over to his writing men; he sent his advertising staff and business representatives to the theatre. Nevertheless, for about six weeks business and receipts rose to £1,774 a week, but then began to diminish.

Writing in *My Northcliffe Diary* under date June 13, 1922, Mr Tom Clarke says: 'Seymour Hicks's daily paragraph about *The Man in Dress Clothes* has got the boot, and I don't suppose Hicks is any too sorry'.

The cancellation of the daily boost was a decision taken by those who perforce removed the Chief's hands from the control of his newspapers. Two months after the entry was made in the diary, Northcliffe was dead. Cochran's comment on Northcliffe's second attempt to make people do as he wished was: 'Of course, Northcliffe was already potty at the time!'

With regard to the faking of the figures when Northcliffe enquired what they were before the *Daily Mail* boost began, Cochran says that eventually he told Northcliffe what he had done and Northcliffe replied: 'You'd have been a damned fool if you hadn't'. To a philosophising moralist there must be a wealth of revelation in those words of the powerful newspaper proprietor.

IT is quite usual for newspapers to maintain in their offices lists of names which are taboo. Names which appear in the lists are those of men and women who have incurred the displeasure of the particular newspaper, either because they have said or written something which is considered detrimental to that particular newspaper, or else it may be the name of somebody who has personally offended the proprietor, his wife, or a friend of either sex. There appeared some little time back on such a list of a London newspaper the name of an Admirable Crichton of the British theatre and the name of a famous musician, also a famous art dealer, now dead. Sometimes names are maintained indefinitely on the list; sometimes it may be a period of weeks or months.

I offer this explanation of normal newspaper routine as a background to the examination of the relations between the subject of this biographical study and a one-time famed leader of the British Bar, the late Sir Edward Marshall Hall, and I would suggest that the evidence shows that in this instance, Northcliffe went beyond the usual routine of having the name of a man who offends a newspaper proprietor placed on the newspaper's black list. The case is one which exhibits Northcliffe as a good hater, as undoubtedly

any man has a right to be if he so chooses, but whether
it is a good cause for a man who owns a powerful
newspaper to use it to persecute a man, of high or
lowly station, is entirely another matter. Sir Max
Pemberton has given the public two pieces of evidence,
purporting to extol Northcliffe's personal courage. In
the first instance it is an account of a thrashing Northcliffe administered in his youth to a 'lout', while in
the second instance it is a case of a man who called on
Northcliffe at Carmelite House with the intention,
according to Pemberton, of blackmailing the Chief.
Northcliffe assaulted the man with a heavy paper-
weight. In the case of Marshall Hall there may well
have been a burst of preliminary fury, but the hate,
although eventually smoothed away, was of long
duration and the tale of it I will no longer delay in
the telling.

In the year 1900 Britain was stirred to the depths
by what was known as the 'Yarmouth Murder'. A man
named H. J. Bennett was arrested for causing the
death of his wife on Yarmouth sands. Marshall Hall,
not then knighted, was briefed for the defence. It was
not disclosed at the Old Bailey trial, but it became
known after Bennett had been sentenced and hanged,
that while he was working in Woolwich Arsenal, he
had acted as a Boer spy. Although the prosecution
alleged that the motive for murder was the accused
man's desire to marry another woman, it was highly
probable that Mrs Bennett's violent death by strangu-
lation was due to the fact that she knew of her husband's guilt, and she had been heard to exclaim: 'I
could get you fifteen years'.

During the sensational trial, Marshall Hall made
violent attacks on the Press. The local newspapers had
attacked Bennett, with the result that feeling was

running high; the defence made application for
Bennett's trial to be transferred from the local Assize
to the Central Criminal Court in London. Certain
London newspapers had interviewed persons who
knew Bennett; their stories had been published. One
sentence Marshall Hall uttered was memorable. He
said: 'Bennett has been tried by his journalistic peers
and found guilty'. It must here be said that one of the
newspapers attacked by Marshall Hall for malpractice
was the *Evening News*, which was the property of
Alfred Harmsworth.

Bennett's trial took place in March 1901, but as it
happened, in July 1900, two months before the murder,
Marshall Hall had appeared in a libel action against
the *Daily Mail*. In those days, the old Gaiety Theatre
in the Strand, London, was the background for beautiful and vivacious women, many of whom married into
the British peerage; one of them was Miss Rosie Boote,
who married the Marquis of Headfort. Another
popular young actress was a Miss Hettie Chattell.
Both these young women were under thirty years of
age. At the time of the libel action, Miss Boote was
engaged and her name and Miss Chattell's were
frequently featured in the popular press. One such
paragraph appeared in the 'Green Room Gossip' in
the *Daily Mail*. In the paragraph it was stated: 'Miss
Rosie Boote, whose name is frequently before the
public just now, is the daughter of Hettie Chattell,
the principal "boy" in the Hippodrome pantomime'.
In view of the importance the Marshall Hall incident
has to this biographical study of Northcliffe, it may
be as well to give a short outline of this 'Green Room
Gossip' feature in the *Daily Mail*.

The column, which appeared on Wednesdays and
Saturdays, was edited by Mr Boyle Laurence who

had a staff of four or five men. The late Sidney Dark, who was a frequent contributor to the column, states in his autobiography that this feature cost a good deal of money. Dark later became a staff reporter on the *Daily Mail*. Both he and Boyle Laurence later joined the *Daily Express*, and Dark, later still, became Editor of the *Church Times*.

The point of the paragraph in the *Daily Mail* which gave rise to the libel action was that Miss Chattell was not the mother of Miss Rosie Boote and that she was actually twenty-eight years of age.

Miss Chattell, naturally, intensely angry, issued a writ for libel; the *Daily Mail* immediately inserted a paragraph apologising for what it called 'our obvious mistake', adding: 'There are many well-known actresses who perform under their maiden names, but the many friends and admirers of Miss Chattell are aware that she is an unmarried lady, and we offer her our sincere apologies.'

It will be noted that the apology does not state that Miss Chattell was twenty-eight, approximately the same age as the other actress of whom the *Daily Mail* had stated that she was the mother. Miss Chattell considered that the original paragraph and apology, read together, might give rise to a very offensive inference, therefore she continued with her libel action, and the *Daily Mail*'s lawyers asked for three weeks' grace in which to deliver a defence. At the end of that period the *Daily Mail* delivered no defence, so the action went forward.

Both sides briefed the leading counsel of the day: for Miss Chattell, Marshall Hall and Mr Montague Lush; for the *Daily Mail*, Mr Horace Avory, K.C., and Mr Arthur Gill.

Marshall Hall attacked the Press and particularly

the *Daily Mail*, alleging that the apology had aggrav-
ated the libel and that the *Daily Mail* had asked for
three weeks' grace in order to make enquiries all over
England about Miss Chattell.

The *Daily Mail* had been asked for the name of
the contributor who had supplied the material for the
paragraph. The newspaper very naturally refused to
disclose the information; honourable newspapers never
do disclose such information, and although Marshall
Hall may not have been aware of the technical build-
up of such columns as the 'Green Room Gossip'
column, it is possible that it was the work of more than
one person. Then Marshall Hall made this statement:
'My client (Miss Chattell) may have to work hard for
a living, but her reputation is entitled to the same
consideration as that of any lady in the land, *including
Mrs Alfred Harmsworth*!'

One can well imagine the scorn and the bitterness
Marshall Hall put into that sentence. Northcliffe, of
course, at that time was plain Alfred Harmsworth.

Marshall Hall asked for heavy damages and the
jury gave Miss Chattell £2,500 damages, actually
£1,500 more than she had claimed. According to Mr
Edward Marjoribanks, Marshall Hall's biographer,
Miss Chattell told her counsel that her grievance was
really only that her age had been misrepresented, but
out of such little drops of water mighty oceans are
made.

After the verdict there came a stormy meeting
between Northcliffe and his legal advisers. The newspaper proprietor was smarting, for two reasons:
Marshall Hall had made a slighting reference to his
wife and he had attacked the *Daily Mail*. Northcliffe
went to Essex Court and consulted one of the greatest
counsel of the day, Sir Edward Clarke. Northcliffe

intimated that he was going to appeal, that he wished an attack to be made on Marshall Hall's conduct of the case, and that he was to be 'taught a lesson'. Northcliffe briefed no fewer than five leading members of the Bar: Clarke, Avory, Charles Gill, Arthur Gill and Walter Frampton.

Clarke demanded a new trial on the ground that the jury had been inflamed by the violent address of Marshall Hall. He also commented on the 'immense verdict' and the 'wonder' how it had been obtained.

The Bench was composed of the Master of the Rolls and Lords Justices Stirling and Mathew. Now it was common knowledge at the Bar and a matter of comment by the first Lord Birkenhead (the famous F. E. Smith) that Lord Justice Mathew disliked Marshall Hall. It seems that a political dispute was behind the frequent scenes in Court between the judge and the advocate; Mathew was an Irishman and a Home-Ruler, whereas Marshall Hall was a Unionist and anti-Home-Ruler. As soon as the hearing of the appeal began, the fight was on.

Lord Justice Mathew said that Marshall Hall's implication that the *Daily Mail* had used the three weeks' grace to search England for things discreditable to Miss Chattell was 'disgraceful'. Marshall Hall said he resented the word 'disgraceful'. All through the hearing Lord Justice Mathew showed his antipathy to Marshall Hall, and when the Master of the Rolls delivered judgement he said that while he had no sympathy with the class of literature complained of, which pandered to the unhealthy taste of the public, and while the anecdote was false in fact and a very grave libel (I am now quoting the Master's actual words), . . . there was no doubt that Marshall Hall's speech had a very serious effect in inflaming the damages and that the verdict ought not to be allowed to stand.

The effect of these words was ruinous to Marshall Hall. The next day *The Times* (which at that moment was *not* in Northcliffe's control) published a leading article censoring Marshall Hall: other newspapers took notice of the matter, perhaps less moderately than *The Times*.

Marshall Hall saw his income at the bar drop from thousands to hundreds. At the time of the appeal (1901) Marshall Hall's income from the Bar was 4,420 guineas; the next year it was 2,099 guineas. In August 1902, he was in serious financial difficulties and was offered financial assistance by Sir Rufus Isaacs. Marshall Hall offered Isaacs his favourite pearl pin as security for a loan of £500. The loan fell through owing to Marshall Hall's pride; the great advocate sold his collection of antique silver and was able to pull through, but there was trouble ahead.

In March 1903, Marshall Hall was briefed in a somewhat unsavoury case which again took him to the Court of Appeal, where he once more fell foul of Lord Justice Mathew. Once again newspaper comment was adverse to the advocate and in 1904 his Bar income dropped to 1,990 guineas, and in 1905, 1,743 guineas. Northcliffe had not forgiven him, and Mr Thomas Marlowe, the Editor of the *Daily Mail*, had said that the Chief was still hostile to him. Marshall Hall complained that when he won a case his name was either not mentioned in the 'Harmsworth Press' or he was referred to as 'Mr Hall'. If he lost a case, however, his full name was given and sometimes it appeared in the headlines. Here is an example: Marshall Hall appeared in a minor action connected with an alleged swindle. Marshall Hall appeared for the defendant, who lost his case, and the plaintiff was awarded £25 damages. The *Daily Mail* headline was: 'A Bit of a Mug—Mr Marshall Hall's Client Loses his Case.'

It is possible that Marshall Hall exaggerated the alleged persecution to which he said he was subjected, but, nevertheless, he wrote to Charles Gill, the eminent barrister, and asked him to intercede on his behalf with Northcliffe. The letter did not, as a matter of fact, immediately follow the 'Bit of a Mug' headline, but after Marshall Hall had appeared in a divorce case which the *Daily Mail* headlined: 'Mr Marshall Hall Again'.

The letter to Gill contained this statement: 'I know, of course, that the hostility of the Editor is due to the fact that I said in the Chattell case that, but for bad editing, those untrue personal paragraphs would not have found their way into print, and I *believe* that the Editor was hauled over the coals for his carelessness. Can you help me to stop this persecution . . .?'

'I can, of course, go to the Chamberlain and tell him and get him to help politically, but I don't want to do this if I can avoid it. I thought you would do something for me with Harmsworth, who, I believe, belongs to the Beefsteak Club. . . .' The 'Editor', of course, was Marlowe, and Marshall Hall was quite wrong in believing that he was the root of the 'persecution'. Whether Charles Gill tried to do anything to help his friend, I do not know, but, if he did, nothing came of it.

In 1905, Marshall Hall appeared for the plaintiff in a libel action against the *Daily Chronicle* and obtained £800 damages for the plaintiff. When Marshall Hall read the account of the action in the *Daily Mail* he saw he was referred to as: 'Mr M   Hall'. The blank space between the 'M' and the 'Hall' was intended in the first place, quite obviously, to have been filled with the word 'Marshall'. Now it is very probable that neither the famous advocate nor his friends knew the technical explanation of that blank space.

At the beginning of this chapter, I explained how and why certain names appear in the black lists of newspapers; it may be reasonably contended that when Northcliffe decided to 'teach Marshall Hall a lesson', he had his name placed on the black lists of the newspapers he controlled. It may be further deduced that with regard to the *Daily Mail*, Northcliffe had given certain instructions as to how reports of cases in which Marshall Hall figured should be displayed. When the report of the *Daily Chronicle* libel action was sub-edited in the *Daily Mail* office, by some mischance the full name of the advocate appeared in the newspaper 'copy'. When the first proof came to the editorial desk, the name Marshall Hall was, by some other mischance, allowed to remain, contrary to the expressed orders of the Chief. When the report came in again in the page proof, the full name was allowed to remain. The page was then cast in the foundry. Then either someone on the editorial desk suddenly remembered the Chief's orders and rushed to the printing plant to have the error corrected, or else the man making up the page caught the error and had the offending word 'Marshall' erased. In any case, the technical procedure is the same: when the page is locked in its frame, the only way to erase an error is to take a chisel and cut away the words in type, and that is why there was a blank space.

Thomas Marlowe and Marshall Hall were both members of the Garrick Club, but were not acquainted. Nevertheless, on February 4, 1905, Marshall Hall wrote

to the Editor of the *Daily Mail* (Thomas Marlowe)
saying he had had his attention called to the report in
the *Daily Mail* of February 3, of the libel action against
the *Daily Chronicle* and that he noticed that for some
reason known only to the *Daily Mail* his name had
been altered, after the type had been set and spaced.
He added that for his part he did not care whether
the paper spelt his name properly or not at all, but
what did matter was that this sort of sub-editing lent
colour to what he had been told was a fact, namely,
that some member of the *Daily Mail* staff had a personal grievance against him. He added that he was
loth to believe this, but he was of the opinion that the
way the *Daily Mail* had treated him during the past
three years showed which way the wind was blowing,
and that anyone on the staff should have taken the
trouble to alter 'Marshall' into 'M' but leave the
valuable spacing showed that an amount of care and
attention was being lavished on his name which were
far in excess of his deserts. Marshall Hall went on to
say that it seemed to him a curious coincidence when
if by any manner of means the report of a case in
which he was engaged could be made to seem to
reflect upon him in the smallest degree, the sub-editing
was always the other way. Then the value of space
meant nothing; one found 'Marshall' in capitals, and
it was thought worth while to print big headlines: 'MR
MARSHALL HALL AGAIN'.

Within a few days the two men met in the Garrick
Club, when the advocate said to the Editor: 'Why is
it that you and Harmsworth have got this down on
me? I don't like to squeal, but the thing has been
going on for years, and I'm being driven out of
business. Surely it can't still be the Chattell case? You
got your own way then.' Marlowe reminded Marshall

Hall of the slighting remark the advocate had made about Mrs Alfred Harmsworth. Marshall Hall said he had forgotten it, and asked what he had better do.

'Well, a gentleman can always apologise', said Marlowe. Marshall Hall wanted to know whether his apology would be accepted. Marlowe replied that it would depend on the terms of the apology. Marshall Hall immediately sat down and drafted a letter which Marlowe said he believed would be in order. The lawyer wrote that he had just been told that Northcliffe was under the impression that something he had said three years ago, in opening the case as counsel for the plaintiff in Chattell *v.* the *Daily Mail*, was intended to cast some reflection upon Lady Northcliffe. Marshall Hall said he was taking the earliest opportunity of expressing his deep regret that anything he said should have been so misunderstood and that he had not the smallest intention of making an aspersion or reflection upon anyone, still less upon a member of Lord Northcliffe's family, and that now that his attention had been called to it, he quite felt that the remark was an unfortunate one to make, and that it would have been better left unsaid.

A personal meeting was arranged, when Northcliffe accepted the apology. Marshall Hall had been 'taught his lesson' and was forgiven.

Two years later Marshall Hall was approached by Northcliffe to make a request to Lord Alverstone (then Lord Chief Justice) with regard to a reprieve for a man named Rayner, the illegitimate son of William Whiteley, who had been found guilty of the murder of his father. This was a case in which Northcliffe for private reasons took a personal interest. Reference to these private reasons is made elsewhere. Later still,

Northcliffe briefed Marshall to defend the *Daily Mail* in sundry actions for alleged libel and slander.

Yes, Northcliffe was a 'good hater', a very human trait. One more instance may be added.

James Bernard Fagan, the playright, wrote a play called *The World*. The chief character was a newspaper proprietor, a character Northcliffe believed was intended to represent himself. Northcliffe did not like it, but there was nothing he could do about it. However, a great deal later, Fagan figured in a divorce case. Northcliffe gave instructions as to how this case should be reported and displayed. He remarked to one of his secretaries: 'Fagan put me on the "boards"; I'm going to put him on the bills!' (newspaper posters).

SINCE Lord Northcliffe died, one woman and six men have published biographies in which he was the centrepiece. A number of autobiographies have made mention of him, and often they were not flattering allusions, but every biographer was at some time or other either in his employ or had other very close ties with him; often, too, the ties were those of affection, real if perhaps sweetened by memories of favours received.

Of the biographers, one, McNair Wilson, was seemingly a friend who, with fulsome praise and no criticism, constructive or otherwise, clouds the lens of his camera. The late Sir Max Pemberton, the friend of approximately a quarter of a century, likewise allowed his critical faculties to be obscured by affection; by scraping back the left leg and bending his back, Sir Max paid tribute to his liege and lord, but gives us a picture lacking life.

Tom Clarke was long a faithful employee of Northcliffe on the *Daily Mail*. He gave us a series of Northcliffian snapshots, close-ups and long-range shots, but few candid camera pictures; those he did provide are good background material for the purposes of biographical study, but they seem to suggest that the photographer was usually too intimidated by his subject to really

do justice to him or to allow posterity to observe more
than a bare outline of the life of a man, who, for good
or ill, had more power to influence mass thought than
any other. Tom Clarke's pictures are human, but
although he succeeded in portraying the *nouveau riche*
side of Northcliffe's character, one cannot help feeling
somewhat sorry for this biographer who was constantly
being reminded by his Chief that even the cigarette
he now held between his lips would cost him nothing,
and when he visited his employer in the South of
France, was offered gratuities in order to go and
gamble at the local Casino. Certainly Clarke had the
grace to relate these stories and anecdotes, which, even
if they may draw unjust attention to the writer himself, do at least provide us with certain angles on the
character of Northcliffe.

It is, one supposes, inevitable that the great and the
near-great attract sycophants even as the flowers
draw the bees, but there the simile must end, for the
bees at least are busy, while the sycophants or 'yes-
men' are more apt to be drones than bees. Undoubtedly Northcliffe attracted the 'yes-men' and
some of them wrote books about him, but no 'yes-man'
was Hamilton Fyfe, who produced the only Northcliffe biography which contains any element of criticism; yet, an otherwise admirable book is marred by
errors of fact which arise either from bias or from lack
of controlled information. Such errors occur in Fyfe's
references to the Northcliffe will and his 'unofficial
family'.

Fyfe's Northcliffe biography was published eight
years after the death of his Chief and dedicated in the
form of a letter to Northcliffe's brother, Harold, the
first Lord Rothermere. Fyfe begins his letter with the
sentence: 'Whether you will like this book I cannot

Lord Northcliffe, and Mr Wickham Steed, Editor of 'The Times', on board the 'Aquitania', July 17, 1921, thirteen months before he died. Lord Northcliffe gave instructions for the picture to be taken and used in the 'Daily Mail' and 'The Times', July 18 'Not less than 4½ inches square'

tell . . .', but there is no reason at all why he should not have liked it, except perhaps for the occasional slipping aside of the curtain to give brief but indiscreet glimpses of Northcliffe's private life. Many people, however, may think that a man who had made it his mission to control mass thought, could not entirely screen his own private life; indeed, he might call himself fortunate if the screen remained standing and did not fall until after his death.

Among the biographies I have listed, I have included one which was unorthodox; it is entitled *Northcliffe's Return*; it was written by Hannen Swaffer, for more than half a century an outstanding figure in British journalism and a man whose sincere belief in spiritualism is as well known as it is uncontested.

During his lifetime Northcliffe's interest in spiritualism can be summed up factually in one sentence: 'What is it worth as a talking point?' Northcliffe, perfectly correctly, as a purveyor of news and views, judged everything, literally *everything*, from the 'talking point' angle. What people want to talk about, they want to read about. Some of Northcliffe's biographers claim for him that he *knew* what people wanted to read. That is sheer nonsense. Ask any honest editor if he *knows* what his readers want. He will tell you that he knows only when the idea has registered; he may try something and find it does not catch on, or, on the other hand, it may, and then and then only does the editor 'know' what the public wants. But who is the public? *The Times* public may want, sometimes, something the *Daily Express* public wants, but it may be only seldom that the *Daily Express* public wants what *The Times* public wants. To return to Northcliffe and spiritualism, it was a 'talking point' like flying, or Standard Bread, or any other well-known North-

M

cliffian 'stunt'. He did at one time toy with the idea of running a serious series of articles by authoritative writers, and he did make a big killing in his *Sunday Dispatch* with a series of articles by the Reverend Vale Owen entitled 'Beyond the Veil'. Northcliffe wanted to pay the clergyman a thousand pounds for the series, but Owen refused to accept any money. After Northcliffe died, the Reverend Vale Owen claimed he had been in contact with Northcliffe, when the former newspaper proprietor expressed his regret that he did not have his cheque book with him.

Since Hannen Swaffer published his Northcliffe book he has had more to say about Northcliffe and the spirit world. Swaffer claims that he is able to contact Northcliffe 'like ringing someone on the telephone'. Swaffer told me that sometimes when he talks with Northcliffe, the Chief is in a very good mood, which old Northcliffians know to mean a teasing mood. Swaffer said that on one particular occasion Northcliffe had said: 'Every time I look at the *Daily Express* I ask myself: "Was your journey really necessary?"'

On the same occasion, which occurred shortly before the death of Lord Southwood, Northcliffe spoke of the *Daily Herald* and said: 'Elias (Southwood's name before he was made a peer) and Dunbar (a high *Daily Herald* executive), they are nothing but a couple of "hams"; not even kosher!'

Swaffer says that Northcliffe in the spirit world has become a Socialist and his conversations sometimes show a certain grimness. Northcliffe is opposed to war, now that he is able to 'view the whole world in true perspective'. Northcliffe told Swaffer: 'I attend the *Daily Mail* editorial conferences and shout in their ears to tell them how wrong they are, but they can't hear me'.

Northcliffe, says Swaffer, suffers now because the

instrument he forged and used for such wrong purposes is still being used for wrong purposes, and he is powerless to make those who control it now use it to further his new ideals.

In connection with Mr Swaffer's statement, the following letter which appeared on November 2, 1953, in the correspondence column of the *Daily Mail* may be found interesting. 'I am a great admirer of the late Northcliffe, whom I remember as a great statesman in his own right, and who without doubt did much to bring the 1914 war to a successful end.'

'Do you know, I often think his spirit helps to direct the "Comment" article; it is always so wise and yet so simply written, and the whole of the paper is such that the most fastidious could not reproach any articles of news. . . .', etc.

Miss Louise Owen, who was an intimate friend and associate of Northcliffe for twenty years, wrote a book entitled *Northcliffe: The Facts*. Although this book contains a good deal of interesting Northcliffian matter, it is, for the most part, a section of the writer's autobiography, consisting largely of an account of a long-drawn-out legal battle Miss Owen fought against Northcliffe's executors. The book gives her own version of why she was defeated; it makes sensational reading and perhaps for this reason the book was published privately and sold privately.

Miss Owen makes the claim that, in 1921, Northcliffe told her she was the most influential woman in Europe; Miss Owen explains this remark by giving her own estimation of Northcliffe's influence in Great Britain and quotes the Chief on her influence with him, which, if one accepts Miss Owen's opinion of Northcliffe's power, supports Northcliffe's statement. Unfortunately, Miss Owen fails to explain to her readers the channels through which she exercised her alleged great influence with Northcliffe. True, she shows that Northcliffe was making her an annual allowance of a little more than £4,000 a year, but she does not clearly explain what services she rendered in return for this not inconsiderable sum. She publishes a few facsimile letters from Northcliffe, one of which begins: 'My dear Lulu', but the others begin with the more staid: 'Dear Miss Owen'.

Miss Owen hints at the great part she played behind the scenes in the period immediately preceding the purchase of *The Times*, but gives no details of any sort. With regard to journalistic matters, Miss Owen avers that she had Northcliffe's authority to order any of his editors to publish any story she desired, likewise she says she had the power to send out any reporter to investigate any story, but, most tantalisingly, she omits to inform her readers whether she ever exercised this authority, and if she did, in what circumstances. Perhaps, however, Miss Owen's most valuable contribution to Northcliffiana is her account of Northcliffe as a family man.

Northcliffe's interest in children and his affection for children is beyond all doubt. In Northcliffe's apartment in *The Times* office he had a cupboard full of toys. 'These are for my nieces and nephews', he said. 'I'm at home to them every Thursday. They come here and take charge of me.' Can anyone imagine a more pathetic figure than this multi-millionaire newspaper owner, controlling *The Times*, the most respected newspaper in the world; the *Daily Mail*, the newspaper with the largest circulation in the United Kingdom; the *Overseas Daily Mail* which carried his 'talking points' to the furthest corners of the earth; the *Continental Daily Mail*, taking them all

over Europe; owner-in-chief of more than three score
and ten weekly and monthly publications, controlling
the mass thoughts of millions, and hungering for dream
children who never came to life?

What a story Northcliffe could have made of his
son, Alfred, the heir who was not an heir, the boy in
whom he put his faith and found himself deceived; but
let Miss Owen tell her own story. Miss Owen, who has
given me permission to quote her, says: 'I will take
you . . . behind the scenes and let you have the facts as
told to me by Lord Northcliffe himself. He became a
father when a mere youth. This marked a crucial epoch
in his life, but it helped to bring to the surface his
exceptional sense of protection of those in need, which
amounted almost to a craving. If ever a man paid in
full for a youthful error, that man was Northcliffe;
it pursued him all his life. But as soon as he was able,
he did his best to rectify it in a manner inconceivable
to the ordinary man of the world. No cant or hypo-
crisy, for he acknowledged to the child—a boy—that
he was his father. He signed his letters to him: "Your
affectionate father", and the boy signed his: "Your
affectionate son".

'Lord Northcliffe's own family and friends, even his
old colleagues, knew of this chapter of his youth, and
one or two of his trusted staff travelled with the boy
to help him gain experience.

'It was a dramatic moment when Lord Northcliffe
first told me this story, and exclaimed: "You know my
son: you have been talking to him this morning". I
hastily made a mental review of my visitors, and then
in a flash I placed him. Without waiting a second, I
walked into my room adjoining, and crossed to the
desk where a young man was awaiting my Chief. I
made a pretence of hurriedly looking for a paper in

order to study him, when my eyes became riveted on his hands. They were identical in shape and size to Northcliffe's, especially his finger-nails. I returned to my Chief's room and said: "Yes, I have seen him", and he appeared relieved, as though a burden had been lifted. He could now talk to me freely about the boy's future.

'I had bought a gold watch at Asprey's for Northcliffe to give the boy on his birthday. I did not at the time suspect the relationship. I just thought he was one of the many young men whom Northcliffe befriended, and I naturally did not disclose to him that I had been made aware of his parentage. He confided to me his hopes and plans for his future, and I remember very clearly his pride when giving me from time to time the little poems he had written.

'The boy had the advantage of a tutor and had been to Cambridge, no expense having been spared by Northcliffe. He then entered Carmelite House, and after gaining a certain amount of experience in different departments, he was moved to another office. The boy often said to me: "You would be surprised if you knew what a wonderful father I have; he really is a great man."

'It was most pathetic to see Northcliffe literally hungering for the affection of this boy. That great paternal love of which he was capable was centred in his son, and Northcliffe was anxious for him to live in a suitable, homely atmosphere. This was the reason for the late Mrs Wrohan's reappearance at the *Daily Mail* office. Northcliffe explained to me: "She is a very lonely woman, and she tells me she can make a home for my boy."

'I had first met her at Carmelite House as far back as November 1902, when she came along to do some typewriting, for which Northcliffe told me to send her a cheque for £25. Thinking the amount excessive, I questioned it, but he replied: "Send it on, she needs it. I knew her years ago." Later he told me that Sutton (Sir George Sutton) was helping her to keep an eye on his boy, which explained the friendship between Sir George Sutton and the late Mrs Wrohan.

'When Northcliffe's son, who by the way was called Alfred, first started work at Carmelite House, he lived in rooms in Temple Chambers. His mother, whom I knew personally, enjoyed a small allowance from Northcliffe, which was paid through a firm of solicitors named Close & Co. Although she had in the meantime married, and had a family, Northcliffe kept her informed, from time to time, of her boy's progress. I remember him sending a little gift to one of her daughters who resembled her half-brother, and because she reminded Northcliffe of his own son he gave her, when she grew up, a position of reader of serials and stories as she had to earn her living.'

'Mrs Wrohan left her small apartment for a suite of rooms at Savoy Court for herself and the boy. He asked my advice, as she wanted him to call her "mother". I told him not to, as his own mother was still living.'

'To Northcliffe's sorrow, his son was not altogether a success. He became extravagant and restless, and disinclined to settle down to real work. My Chief was very distressed, for he truly loved him; he was part of him, and he would have kept him at his side. He left England and has lived in Australia ever since, not in luxury, but in simple surroundings.' He died sometime since.

'When my thoughts go back to the past, one scene remains in my mind as clear as crystal. Lord Northcliffe, in a reflective mood, told me how all his plans, all he had hoped to do in connection with his son, had miscarried. Suddenly, to my consternation and dismay, he buried his face in his hands and wept. No words of mine can convey my feelings at that moment, to see this man, whom the world looked upon as hard, ruthless, ambitious and dictatorial, turning to me and unburdening himself of his secret sorrow.'

'Some time after the boy had gone abroad, Northcliffe was discussing with me the distribution of his wealth. His son was ruled out as heir, as Northcliffe said more money would destroy him, and he had provided most generously for his relatives. He intended that his godson, Alfred Pemberton, son of Sir Max, should inherit his fortune, but later he dismissed that idea. He then told me of a certain baby boy who had just been adopted by Mrs Wrohan. "At one time I though to make him my heir", he said, "but the question of religion is against that; he is being brought up as a Roman Catholic, and the Marquis of Bute is this child's godfather."

'Some time after, Mrs Wrohan adopted two more babies. To keep in the limelight she would hint that Northcliffe was the father of these three children and that she was the mother—thus one can trace how this particular story originated.

'Lord Northcliffe heard the gossip, and in speaking to me, said: "Do you really believe she is busy dropping babies about? Don't be so stupid. Have you forgotten her age? I remember telling you the history of the boy, and when you next go to Paris, Mr ——, also Dr ——, will tell you the identity of the other two children, and don't forget she says she is a widow!"

'I remember he laughingly added: "I am, according to some, a real Don Juan. If I were to take notice of all the ladies with whom my name is bracketed, I should not have a second left to look after my business." His staff knew that he worked eighteen hours a day.'

'He again repeated the real facts of the parentage of these children, and the reason the boy had two companions. I have conclusive proof that neither Lord Northcliffe nor the late Mrs Wrohan were their parents.'

'I was surprised and shocked to hear responsible men and women repeating this idle silly gossip, and at the same time crawling and cringing to obtain the favour of the man they were openly vilifying. Unfortunately, these scandals are still repeated, but I am positive Northcliffe won't mind—he loved children.'

'Mrs Wrohan died in July 1923, in a nursing home at Broadstairs under tragic circumstances, surrounded by a veil of mystery. Dr Seymour Price came specially from town to sign the death certificate. Although Mr Montague Ellis, her solicitor, attended her funeral, he could not furnish the Registrar with any information whatsoever as to her real identity, or that of her husband, or whether he was alive or dead.'

'Her will makes interesting reading, for, as already stated, she was poor and unknown when I first met her. In a codicil, Mr Montague Ellis (solicitor to Sir George Sutton) benefited by an annuity of £3,000 free of tax and super-tax, practically absorbing the residue. When he dies it passes to his son.'

'Mrs Wrohan had originally bequeathed to Mr Montague Ellis an annuity of £400, which, one month after Northcliffe's death, was increased to £3,000.'

Miss Owen's statements concerning the son, Alfred, make clear and reasonable Northcliffe's interest in trying to obtain a reprieve for Rayner who was tried and found guilty of the murder of his father, William Whiteley.

Mr Bernard Falk has written considerably about
Lord Northcliffe. Mr Falk relates that Northcliffe
wrote as he spoke, on the spur of the moment, and
without a single eye to posterity, but yet he would have
relished a rounded biography of himself written when
he was alive. He agreed with Lords Brougham and
Carson that a full-dress biography was possible in
one's lifetime. When Northcliffe died, a monumental
history of Alfred Harmsworth, first Baron Northcliffe,
was in course of preparation. Various intimate friends
regarded as suitable as authors had been induced to
try their hand at recording the story of his eventful
life. In one book of journalistic memoirs, the number
of would-be Northcliffe biographers is given as four.

The late H. W. Wilson of the *Daily Mail*, who was
among the many biographers chosen by the Chief,
agreed with Falk that forty draft biographies were
written.

H. W. Wilson was once the Naval Correspondent of
the *Daily Mail*, with which he had a long career in
varied capacities. He comes of a journalist family, and
one of his brothers, J. B. Wilson, was for many years
News Editor of the *Daily Express*.

Once, when Northcliffe was reading one of the
potential biographies, he asked an intimate, with great
bitterness: 'Is that all they can say about me?'

No clue is given as to the identity of this particular
biographer who failed, in Northcliffe's estimation, to
make the grade, but Sir Max Pemberton relates how
he himself during Northcliffe's lifetime tried to write
a biography of his Chief and he tells how difficult the
task was, because Northcliffe's memory was failing
and he transposed the times of the various incidents.
Pemberton quotes one particular incident which
illustrates his point: how Northcliffe muddled the

dates of the periods during which he attended two schools.

Once at Elmwood Northcliffe pointed to a spot near the centre of the garden, exclaiming in an assumed voice of piercing melancholy: 'Shall I tell you what is buried there? Under the earth is buried my life.' He was not exaggerating. A servant, ordered to 'lose' one of the forty 'lives' that had not found favour in his master's sight, had chosen interment for the manuscript as the most merciful form of extinction. Falk comments: 'The incident, rich in melodramatic details, would have made a suitable chapter for an Emily Brontë novel.'

It may be a matter for debate whether the servant on his own initiative buried the MS. of the biography in his master's garden, or whether the master himself gave the instructions, because the master had a curious sense of humour: a very personal sense of humour. But again, why was it necessary to 'lose' any particular MS. of biography, if, as we are told, there were thirty-nine others which failed to find favour? And again, why was it necessary to bury the MS.? Would not death by fire have sufficed?

A close study of the fate of things which Northcliffe ordered should be written and which when written disappeared from sight, never to be seen again, reveals some kink in Northcliffe's character. For instance, when Northcliffe purchased *The Observer* he commissioned a member of the *Daily Mail* staff to write the history of the famous Sunday newspaper. The writing of the history occupied six months. The MS. was handed to Northcliffe and nothing more was heard of it.

Some compilers of those of the forty biographies which did see the light of day mention various aspects

of the Chief's conception of humour. Mr R. D.
Blumenfeld said Northcliffe's sense of humour was
generally under control; Blumenfeld probably learned
to know the times when this sense of humour was not
under control, but Northcliffe's flair both for the
melodramatic and for self-dramatisation turned this
sense of humour into unordinary channels. We read
of his 'sense of mischief', of his love of mystification,
suggestions of schoolboy humour, and there have been
attempts to portray him as a sort of Peter Pan, but, as
Northcliffe was apt to say, sometimes, 'That bird won't
fly'. I think there is evidence that the Northcliffian
sense of humour was very Edwardian—the sort of
thing that had its heyday when Northcliffe's friend and
admirer, Dame Nellie Melba, was in her prime. It was
the day of the hoax, of rather cruel humour; the
elaborated booby trap. Gentlemen thought little of
applying blacking to the rim of a lavatory seat;
apple-pie beds at country house parties were *de
rigueur*. It was a parallel to the throwing of custard
pies and the slipping on a banana skin. I am not
suggesting for one moment that Northcliffe ever took
part in hoaxes, but his sense of humour, sometimes
referred to as 'teasing', often meant barbed remarks
aimed at such persons as Scotsmen and Jews and made
at luncheon or dinner tables. The objects of these
barbed shafts were usually his employees, which prevented anything like spirited repartee. A favourite
Northcliffe sally at a man with a very Scottish name
was: 'You must be a Jew, you have such a Scottish-
sounding name'. Not a very nimble wit, perhaps, but
Edwardian humour was more broad than deep, and
it most certainly was not light and airy.

While writing this biographical study I have sought
for some particularly witty remark which might have

been preserved for posterity, but my search has been in vain. Bernard Falk, when recording his regret at Northcliffe's death, writes: 'We laughed so much together', but one can find no trace of any humour in the records. True, one finds Northcliffe setting a booby trap of telephone wires in a Riviera hotel and of Falk tripping over them, and Northcliffe commenting: 'I knew you would fall over them, but I did not think you would do it so soon.'

Another anecdote refers to an afternoon call Falk paid on his Chief. Northcliffe said to the butler 'in a stage whisper: "Lock up the spoons; *he* has arrived".' Perhaps readers will find these remarks funnier than I do, but I will try once again. Falk is again calling on his Chief. He finds written on a slip of paper lying across a box of cigars: 'Do not steal'.

Perhaps—I do not know—Falk is pulling his readers' legs. I submit this suggestion because I found in Falk's biography a full-length photograph of Arnold Bennett, but all that Falk has to tell us about the famous author is that: '. . . I patronised the same barber's shop as the fastidious Arnold Bennett, whose dressy appearance was matched by scrupulous attention to the care of his face, hands and hair. It has happened that we have been accommodated in adjoining chairs. . . . As we swung together in our respective chairs, heads almost touching, I would observe with unholy pride, that, in the sweeping up, his shorn locks were being indiscriminately mingled with mine. . . .'

Falk gives no other reason why Bennett is dragged into his memoirs.

What Bernard Falk does not tell us about Arnold Bennett is that the great novelist-playwright was himself much intrigued by the character of Northcliffe, and he put him in one of his plays. We have Bennett's

own record (*French Journal*) of his reactions to Northcliffe when he was Alfred Harmsworth. 'I had a notion
of writing a play about him. Of course, I greatly
admired him as a Leviathan, although I never set
eyes on him save occasionally at lunch in the Temple
Restaurant.' Obviously the idea remained with
Bennett for many years; finally Bennett wrote a play
entitled, *What the Public Wants*, which was produced
by Denis Eadie at the Royalty Theatre, London.
Northcliffe was the newspaper proprietor in the play,
which was not an outstanding success.

Northcliffe's former chemistry master, H. G. Wells,
wrote a book, *The New Machiavelli*, in which Northcliffe figured. Wells and Northcliffe were never good
friends, although when the Chief was Director of
Propaganda against Enemy Countries, he made Wells
Director of Propaganda against Germany, but Wells
soon resigned. Wells could not reconcile the views of
Northcliffe as head of the Northcliffe Press and the
views of Northcliffe as chief of the Propaganda service.
In the latter post Northcliffe was making promises to
the Germans, but in his newspaper he was uttering
threats. In both posts Northcliffe was perfectly
sincere, but Northcliffe cared nothing for logic, and
this the coldly scientific brain of Wells could not
understand. During the Washington Naval Conference
Wells was engaged by Northcliffe to write articles for
the *Daily Mail*; the two men quarrelled again because
of Wells' attitude to French policy. Wells left the *Daily
Mail* and he and his articles were taken over by
Beaverbrook in the *Daily Express*.

The relations between Beaverbrook and Northcliffe
were superficially friendly, but undoubtedly Northcliffe resented the successful drive Beaverbrook was
making with the *Daily Express*, which began to threaten

the supremacy of the *Daily Mail*. The late 'Skipper' Williams, an English journalist who worked for the *New York Times*, told me this story. 'Once during the war (the first World War) I was dining with Northcliffe at the Berkeley. A page brought in Beaverbrook's card with a message that he would like to see Northcliffe for a few minutes. "Do you think we ought to receive him?" Northcliffe asked me, adding: "Well, I suppose we should!" ' A superb piece of Irish blarney.

During the first World War Allied newspaper circles were constantly tickled with tales of Northcliffe's alleged two German aunts. The following story, possibly *ben trovato*, was told of an alleged conversation between Beaverbrook and Northcliffe. 'Are you going to print this story about my two German aunts?' asked Northcliffe.

'Certainly not', answered Beaverbrook, 'but, by the way, you might give instructions to have that Hyde Park orator of yours stopped making remarks about my German Editor.' The then Editor of the *Daily Express* was R. D. Blumenfeld, a British naturalised American-born subject of German descent. He told me the story.

Alphonse Courlander wrote a Fleet Street novel entitled *Mightier than the Sword*. One of the characters, a newspaper proprietor, was drawn from the combined characters of Lord Northcliffe and Sir Arthur Pearson, but Northcliffe took it to be a portrait of himself; in this instance he was not annoyed and contented himself with the remark that the portrait was not a bit like. In other cases he was very angry indeed. *Napoleon of the Press* so angered him that he caused all the copies to be bought up and destroyed.

Keble Howard wrote a fulsome novel about Northcliffe, entitled *Lord London*, but this did not please

him; he thought it was intended to be satirical, yet
Keble Howard (Warren Bell) was also the author of
such sentimental novels of London life as *The Smiths of
Surbiton*. He was also 'Chicot' of *The Sketch* and I do not
believe he had a vein of satire in him.

The fact of the matter is: Northcliffe's character was
so complex, so many-sided, that it was literally an
impossibility to make a novel or a play out of him. No
wonder then that there was nothing written during
his lifetime which could please him. Just take this one
instance of his complex and complicated nature. In
the *Daily Mail* he supported the Bill to abolish the
killing of birds to make ornaments of the feathers for
women's hats. Yet we find Mr Hamilton Fyfe recording
this horrible story: '. . . one day on the seashore near
Elmwood, his house on the coast of Kent, he struck
down a seagull with a heavy stick which he carried
and beat it furiously as it lay on the sand. The friend
who was with him saw in this act . . . a sinister symptom
of a disturbed mental balance.'

No, one must give it up; forty lives or four hundred
biographies, it matters not. The Colossus of Fleet
Street was too big a subject for a single biography,
whether written to please him or posterity. Therefore
I am pleased to offer this mere study in biography.

THOSE to whom Northcliffe is a name and not a memory can only with difficulty be brought to believe that once upon a time such a man meant so much to so many people. References to him as 'the uncrowned king of England' and 'the most powerful man in England' must sound empty and foolish today; whether he was ever one or the other depends principally on a point of view, but the point of view itself can only really be correctly focussed by making up one's mind as to the power of the Press.

A newspaper can enlighten or it can inflame public opinion. There are in Great Britain few daily newspapers which can be classed as organs of enlightenment, and those which are in this category possess comparatively low circulations. Put in another way, the newspapers which inflame thought are those with the biggest circulations. Many people believe, I think wrongly, that it would be possible for all newspapers to enlighten their readers and that it is not at all necessary to inflame their opinions. If one looks at the matter from the angle of morality, such a contention cannot be refuted, but human nature being what it is, I do not think such a thing, however desirable it may be, is possible. If every newspaper agreed that henceforth nothing inflammatory would be published, the

N

task of enlightenment would be easy, but if, say, there were one hundred newspapers in Great Britain and ninety-nine of them agreed on a policy of enlightenment, you would nevertheless find that the odd one pretty soon would achieve the largest circulation in the country. Readers of newspapers, that is to say the majority of readers, do not seek enlightenment; they seek entertainment, and the newspaper which provides the best entertainment achieves the biggest circulation. These things Northcliffe found out for himself and he built up his publications on his knowledge. When Northcliffe purchased control of *The Times* he was fully conscious that his ideas, so far as that particular newspaper was concerned, would have to be restrained within certain limits, yet, as will have been seen, it came about that again and again his ideas as to driving force ran counter to the knowledge of the limitations imposed by tradition.

Northcliffe was not a traditionalist; history meant little or nothing to him; he sought to write history, not to learn from it. To him his own methods were the best, although he did say on many occasions that he had learned considerably from the New York *World*.

The tragedy of Northcliffe was the decline of his mental powers before posterity could judge the full stature of his greatness. However, more than thirty years have passed since he died, and by sifting the evidence of what Northcliffe achieved during his career and applying that to what he might have done had he retained his full mental powers, we can reach judgement.

If we agree that Northcliffe's career stands only on his place in British life as a great owner of newspapers, and that he did not figure as a politician, a statesman or an orator, it must be conceded that his power to excite, control or inflame mass thought came from his ownership of *The Times*, the most respected paper in the world, the *Daily Mail*, the morning paper with the then biggest circulation in the United Kingdom, the *Evening News*, the newspaper of the night with the biggest circulation in London, and the *Weekly Dispatch*, a widely read Sunday newspaper. A very strong combination indeed, and a stout platform from which to preach.

The ownership of such a group of newspapers involves tremendous responsibility to shareholders, but responsibilities react in different ways on different men. It might be that some men would accept—nay, seek—the advice of their editors, and be guided by them in the formation of policies, but such procedure was not in Northcliffe's nature. He imposed his own policies, and these policies were usually policies of attack; he was stronger as a prosecutor than as a defender. In the chapter, 'Northcliffe Goes to War', we have seen how he alternately boosted and attacked Lloyd George. Lloyd George in his own memoirs has told how Northcliffe's impetuosity led to distrust. We have seen, too, how Northcliffe boosted Kitchener for the War Office and then sought to drive him out. French and Haig, Cardona and Asquith were all gods at one moment and 'contemptibles' the next. There seemed to be an entire lack of impartial judgment in relation to national affairs, a state of mind perhaps natural to a man who cared more for results than how these results should be attained. 'Do it; do it now' was his motto, a motto well enough in the conduct of commercial enterprises such as national newspapers, but dangerous in the conduct of national affairs, and particularly so in time of crisis.

It is obvious that any man owning a newspaper with

a large national circulation must be a man with whom
the Government of his country is concerned; how much
more so then when a man owns several newspapers of
such calibre. It remains to be said, nevertheless, that
perhaps Governments are sometimes inclined to lose
their sense of perspective and proportion and pay too
much heed to the personal opinions of newspaper
proprietors and the newspapers themselves which are
the mirrors of their proprietors' opinions. It is equally
true that sometimes newspaper proprietors over-
estimate their own importance within the framework
of the national life of their country. Vanity is a human
trait which feeds on the adulation of time-servers. One
needs to be a man of true greatness to withstand the
outside forces driving inwards. Was Northcliffe a man
of such true greatness?

His difficulty was to find a correct balance between
himself as a newspaper proprietor and himself as a
man with great opportunities. Divorced from his
newspapers, Northcliffe lacked the power that might
have come from himself alone. In point of fact,
Northcliffe never was entirely divorced from his newspapers; his oft-repeated references to 'my dear work'
meant his work as the driving force behind his newspapers, and nothing else.

Soured by disappointment that he was not offered
the Premiership of Great Britain, Northcliffe's life
began to lose pattern and design. Even had his mental
powers not collapsed, the disappointment and the
bitterness would have remained, but if his physical and
mental health had not been impaired, one must
consider it possible that time would have softened the
blow, which, like other men in similar circumstances,
Northcliffe attributed to ingratitude.

If in 1922 time had begun to heal the blow of

disappointment, what part would Northcliffe have played in the national life of his country?

We have seen how, even before Northcliffe died, Beaverbrook's *Daily Express* was making the *Daily Mail* extend itself. One may be certain then that Northcliffe would have fought back and would have extended his own genius as a purveyor of news and views. Who would have won the battle? One may be sure that Northcliffe's inventive powers in creating striking 'talking points' would not have lost their vitality, but a more fascinating problem is to try and solve this puzzle: what attitude would Northcliffe have adopted towards Britain's part in international affairs?

Northcliffe's attitude towards Germany can safely be put into two compartments, his personal attitude, which was never very clearly defined, and the attitude of the newspapers he controlled. Of the contents inside the second compartment there can be little doubt. Northcliffe may be called a Jingo, but it was healthy Jingoism; it was the Jingoism of Disraeli, and something which had its roots deep in British soil. When Germany began to kick over the Republican traces, when Adolf Hitler appeared on the international horizon, would Northcliffe have extended the welcome his brother Harold did? I suggest that there is ample evidence to show that he would not have done so. Northcliffe the 'Jew-baiter', as Mr Tom Clarke calls him, might not have been moved by Hitler's diabolic persecution, but I suggest that the readers of the Northcliffe newspapers would not have been told what a fine and sincere gentleman Hitler was.

It is possible that such tactics, which with my imagination I am attributing to a Northcliffe of un-impaired mental power, might have created difficulties with the British Government of the day, because, as usual, Britain would not have been prepared for war, and it is possible that, willy-nilly, Britain might have been forced into war; but would not Britain have been better placed to fight before all the Nazi poison had been instilled into German veins?

To revert to the *Daily Mail* as it might have been if Northcliffe had lived, would reporters like Mr Ward Price have written in the pages of the paper such laudatory articles about Hitler and Mussolini?

Supposing there had been no outbreak of war before Hitler reached his zenith of power, would not North-cliffe have campaigned to put out Neville Chamberlain and put in Winston Churchill? If such a campaign had been successful, that might well have caused war with Germany, but would not war even then have been better than war later?

Supposing that the Churchill campaign had failed and that Neville Chamberlain had remained in office; would there have been a Munich Agreement? I think there would not; I think there might not have been a war, or alternatively, a war fought on more equal terms, because Britain would have been aroused. I do not think the British Union of Fascists would have received such favourable notices in the *Daily Mail* if Northcliffe had been able to carry on.

I am perfectly aware that the things I have been suggesting may rightly be called matters of an in-flammatory nature, but I have already sought to show the impossibility of impressing certain things on the masses without the aid and assistance of strong-arm measures. The question is: when are such measures desirable and when are they not? My own conception of the matter is that an awakened Britain may well be the best safeguard against war; a Britain doped with 'Hitler Wants Peace' is a Britain which is a danger to peace; a potential for war. Yet if Britain dozes and war comes, then there also comes the true test of greatness for a man of Northcliffe's stature.

If Northcliffe in 1939 had been the Northcliffe of 1914, what would his attitude have been? Could it have been said of him, as it was of the Bourbons, that he learned nothing and forgot nothing?

In 1939 Britain was faced with the same dangers as in 1914, but the dangers were more immediate. It was of vital importance that a strict Press censorship should be imposed. Northcliffe, as we have seen, fought that censorship tooth and nail. Either he did not understand or he did not want to understand the vital things which necessitated a censorship.

In 1939 Northcliffe would have been seventy-four years of age. All his working life he stressed the importance of putting youth at the helm, but one fails to notice old age voluntarily giving place to youth. Does age bring wisdom? There is no proof that it does, therefore it might well be possible that a seventy-four-year-old Northcliffe would have made the same errors of judgment as the Northcliffe of forty-nine.

Would we have seen Northcliffe then tilting at the Government, insisting that his correspondents be granted the fullest facilities to report the war? I think that is just what we would have seen. Would we have seen Northcliffe campaigning for this or that Minister to be removed? I think that is just what he would have done. Would he have campaigned to have Montgomery put in charge, and then have campaigned to have him removed? I think that is highly possible. After all, history does repeat itself.

There would most undoubtedly have been much friction between Northcliffe and the country's leaders. I can well imagine that Northcliffe would, *malgré lui*, have become a menace to Great Britain, but I am equally of the opinion that Northcliffe, had he lived on, would have been the one man who, once again *malgré lui*, might have prevented the second World War.

CHAPTER XIII   *Did He Get What He Wanted?*

THE pursuit of happiness is for us mortals a chase
after a quarry few of us ever overtake. If happiness be contentment, then most of us are like the happy
man who possessed no shirt. We are happy because we
are contented, but we do not realise our happiness
and so do not give thanks for it, which may be all for
the best. If a man obtains all he wants, he should be
happy, but it is doubtful whether many men ever
reach the bull's-eye of their life's target. Perhaps they
aim too high, or the target is too far away. Happiness
is an elusive nymph, slipping away when we sometimes
believe we are about to clasp her in our arms.

The lives of ordinary individuals are private lives,
and the scrutiny of them should not be our affair; the
lives of public men cannot stay screened. It is difficult
and perhaps impossible to divide the strictly private
from the public life. The two lives merge into one.
This is particularly the case in the instance of the
subject of my biographical study. Did he reach the
bull's-eye of his life's target? Did he get what he
wanted? To the general public alive during his own
lifetime, Harmsworth-Northcliffe must have been an
unqualified success, a man to be both admired and
envied. In the United States, during the last ten years
of his life, the prestige and fame of Northcliffe were

as high as in his own country; perhaps even higher, because the Americans adore a 'go-getter'. In British circles of wide dimensions a man who is a 'go-getter' is often regarded as a vulgarian, which Northcliffe was not. He was, indeed, the almost perfect example of a plutocrat: a Great Barbarian if you will, a man always prepared to back his own opinions, most often impatient and intolerant of the opinions of others. Threaded through his complicated character were streaks of gentleness, which were visible to the few and not to the many who regarded him as a bully and a tyrant, which he was sometimes. To try to understand the nature of such a man it is essential to avoid judging him as an entity; one must separate as far as is humanly possible the segments of his life, and then, afterwards, try to put them together again. First, then, the man himself.

The outstanding element in his human character was his worship of his mother, who, he often said, was his most exacting critic. In the jargon of today, Northcliffe had a mother-fixation, which to me has a horrible sound. I would prefer to stress the love and affection which linked the son to his mother and she to him. The world did not know and never can know in the fullest measure to what extent she influenced his life and actions. Wherever it was possible, they either met every day or telephoned to each other. When this was not feasible, Northcliffe wrote or cabled his mother every day, and this continued throughout his life and until his fatal illness, when personal communication was impossible. Then Mrs Harmsworth, his mother, had special prayers offered daily for his recovery in a church at High Barnet, near where she was living. As Northcliffe progressed in worldly wealth, his mother's lot became richer, and in the Northcliffe will which made so much commotion in the Law Courts, Mrs Harmsworth's interests were fully protected.

Northcliffe was proud of his family. It is possible that his brothers would have made their own way in the world without his influence and assistance, and would have achieved the wealth and position which became theirs, but it is necessary in this book to record that Northcliffe did indeed give his family, particularly his brothers, all the benefit of his position. One exception must be made; he had no need to help his brother Harold, the first Lord Rothermere; indeed, the shoe was on the other foot. It was Harold who helped Alfred, Lord Northcliffe, and yet if Alfred had not started *Answers*, the first stepping-stone to fame and fortune, and persuaded Harold to give up his safe clerkship and join him in his great adventure, Harold's financial genius might well have lain fallow and would have been wasted. Together they proved an unbeatable team of two, but separately it is doubtful whether the world would have heard much of the one or the other.

In the *History of The Times* you will find these words: 'Northcliffe was a failure in his private life, a greater failure in his public life. Success at his trade came too early. Well before fifty he was far too fond of his own way, and far too certain of getting it at Carmelite House and Fleetway House to be able to tolerate the compromises and delays of politics, or to have a chance of succeeding in a Ministry.'

As a husband, Northcliffe's family life was spoilt, so far as one is able to judge, by the lack of children. Northcliffe, as we have seen, adored children. It has been affirmed that Northcliffe was a man of high moral character, that he abhorred the use of foul language and the abuse of liquor. Despite his Irish hot

temper, none of his close associates heard him use bad
language. This is in striking contrast to two of his con-
temporary newspaper proprietors, both deceased;
both these two men, one a life-long total abstainer,
used the most foul language.

Northcliffe drank in moderation, until the beginning of the last phase. During the war, when he was
head of the British Mission in the United States,
Northcliffe's weary brain felt the need of stimulants.
While making speeches he had in front of him and
drank from what his audiences thought was a glass of
water. It was neat gin.

When the madness was on him, during his last days
in France, just before his male nurses took him back to
London to die, he was drinking heavily, but he did
not know what he did.

Secondly, Northcliffe the newspaper proprietor.

True, Northcliffe began his newspaper career in an
epoch of golden opportunity, but that same opportunity was there for others to exploit, yet they did not.
Northcliffe had imitators, but none blazed the trail
before him. In the telling, the story of Northcliffe's
success may sound simple, but it is necessary to avoid
over-simplification. It was not easy to persuade hard-
bitten financiers to invest their money in a new enterprise such as Northcliffe had in mind. True again that
Northcliffe did not invent; George Newnes founded
Tit-Bits, from which Northcliffe copied his *Answers*,
after tacking down-stream with an unseaworthy craft
called *Answers to Correspondents*. We have seen how this
failed to attract, so that its owner, the young Alfred
Harmsworth, had to dress his little craft, which was
painted orange, much like his rival, the green-hued
Tit-Bits. But the young man was not content merely
to follow a model; he improved on his model and then

branched out into cheap comics, and amassed enough
money to buy a derelict London newspaper and make
of it a sensational success. Then came the greatest *coup*
of all; something that, if he had never created anything
else, would have placed Northcliffe's name in a niche
of fame; the creation and launching of the halfpenny
Daily Mail.

It is true, again, that the *Evening News*, the derelict
evening newspaper, was brought to Northcliffe on a
silver platter by the soured and disillusioned Kennedy
Jones, that ingrown man of Glasgow in whose veins
flowed ink and in whose keen brain were stored the
secrets of success which could be turned into newspaper fortunes. Northcliffe could well have failed in
his mission to conquer the British newspaper world if
'K.J.' had not been at his side.

The *Daily Mail* was the success that Northcliffe fore-
saw it would be; he never had any doubts about it.
He never doubted and his plans were always successful, except once. Northcliffe planned and launched a
daily newspaper edited by women for women, but the
women did not want it; they would not have it—even
at the cost of a halfpenny. What did Northcliffe do?
He turned his women's morning newspaper into a
smart 'snappy' (England did not yet know the word)
illustrated morning newspaper for everybody, and
once again Fortune smiled.

In Fleetway House, Farringdon Street, London,
were the headquarters of the weeklies and monthlies
that Northcliffe created for boys and girls and for
grown-ups too. There were papers for typists and
cyclists; there were papers that long before the films
brought romance into drab lives. Northcliffe had an
inexhaustible bag of ideas and they all brought in
money. It is nonsense to pretend that anyone can know

what people 'wanted to read'. His genius as a purveyor
of reading entertainment far exceeded a puerile claim
to occult knowledge. Northcliffe possessed what is
known as the 'common touch'. He knew that the
majority of his countrymen and countrywomen led
drab and humdrum lives—and in the hey-day of his
success, life in Britain was more humdrum than it is
today. Northcliffe never crusaded for Uplift or
Culture. People wanted romance, excitement, entertainment, and he gave it to them in full measure.
Many a man has earned undying fame for achieving
far less.

Thirdly, the man of affairs.

Northcliffe did not possess the 'money instinct'.
There is all the evidence necessary to prove that he
cared little or nothing for the amassing of wealth for
its own sake. He was extremely generous and it was a
pity that he seldom troubled to see that his generous
impulses were carried out by others in the letter as
well as in the spirit which moved him. In his complicated character there were streaks of cruelty as well as
gentleness, and it is unfortunate that these streaks of
cruelty were often more apparent to the many than
the streaks of gentleness too often apparent only to the
few; but Northcliffe was never mean. His gestures were
generous, whether they were applied to persons or to
affairs. In the building up of his colossal Press Empire,
it was no doubt unavoidable that individuals suffered,
often unjustly.

Fourthly, Northcliffe the politician.

We recall how, early in his career, Northcliffe, as
the young Alfred Harmsworth, contested Portsmouth
and failed to win the seat. Later in life he often
expressed his scorn of politicians, but he never properly
understood politicians, neither did he have any real

conception of statesmanship. It has been said on his behalf that he distrusted politicians because their ways were not his ways; that he was too direct in his methods and could not abide the more tortuous minds of politicians. That I do not think is the entire truth.

Northcliffe was no master of logical thinking; to him thought and action were linked; to think was to act on the thought. He simply could not understand that statecraft was not, and never could be, direct action. Neither could he abide the delegation of authority; men had to do as they were told; they must never argue. 'Theirs was not to reason why.' 'I'm not arguing with you, young man', he used to say, 'I'm telling you!' He was amazed and angered when any 'young man' had the temerity to express concern with the reason of an order. This was all very well in his business, but he was too impetuous, too hasty in his judgement of politics, to achieve even the smallest success in that difficult arena.

Many instances can be cited to point a moral to this story. Some instances have already fallen into their proper categories during the recital of this biographical study, but there are still others. Let us examine just a few of them.

Northcliffe's political judgement was hopelessly at fault when he tried to lead the country during the Joseph Chamberlain Tariff Reform campaign. The truth is that he never really understood the significance of the campaign; to him it was not so much a political campaign likely to affect the lives of every man in the country. Rather was it a newspaper 'stunt', a 'talking point', something to make the people read his newspaper. He never grasped that here he was faced with something fundamental, something that touched the deeply rooted prejudices of the then British way of

living. As a result, he guessed wrongly, was hopelessly
at sea as to what was going on and—lost his temper! A
way he had when sometimes things happened that
were too big for him, too big in the sense that they
were outside the realm of newspapers, and he never
really believed that anything could be outside the
realm which encompassed the whole of his own life.

Towards the end of that life, Northcliffe ran a
campaign in the *Daily Mail*, the *leit-motif* of which was:
'Hats off to France'. Northcliffe was on friendly
terms with the old 'Tiger', Georges Clemenceau, but
at the time of the campaign, Clemenceau's arch-
enemy, Raymond Poincaré, was Prime Minister in
France, and Poincaré was a *sujet difficile*. Relations
between Britain and her wartime ally France were not
so good. It is possible that Clemenceau had no
illusions about Northcliffe's status in British political
life, but Poincaré had; he thought Northcliffe was all-
powerful in Britain. Now Northcliffe had since his
early days spent a considerable part of his time in
France; he liked the country and he liked the people.
He knew France as many wealthy Englishmen of his
time knew the country; he liked to play golf there; he
had a villa on the Riviera; he liked to relax there—
or relax as much as a man of his terrific activity could
relax anyway. But he did not *know* France. He was
unable to appreciate or understand the intricate
interplay of Anglo-French relations, the clash of
British and French interests in the Near East and elsewhere. Consequently, the *Daily Mail*'s 'Hats off to
France' campaign was a source of embarrassment to
the British Government and did far more harm than
good.

Then there is the instance of the mysterious alleged
interview Northcliffe was said to have given, and

The Times

(*The Fiend*) '*Welcome, Great Master! From you we shall at last learn the Science of Lying!*' From '*Simplicissimus*'—*Munich*

which, for the first time in British history, caused a statement to be read in the House of Commons linking the King to a newspaper. This story is perhaps best told in the words of Sir George Arthur, already mentioned in his role of secretary to Lord Kitchener, but Sir George was later secretary to Queen Alexandra and so has the right to express his views concerning Northcliffe and the son of Queen Alexandra: King George V.

Sir George Arthur writes: 'Early in July (1921) Lord Northcliffe—the darling of journalistic fortune, but who had never enjoyed the breezes of Court favour—started on a world tour which he fondly believed would stir the world to its depths. For some time there had been circulated in American newspapers assertions to the effect that the King (George V) was taking a line of his own with regard to Ireland, and it was confidently added by some more enterprising gentlemen that the Belfast speech had been made without consulting the British Cabinet. Lord Northcliffe, who had made America the first stage of his Odyssey, was now credited with the statement that the King has asked Mr Lloyd George (the Premier): "Are you going to shoot all the people in Ireland? You must come to some agreement with them. I cannot have my people killed in this fashion".'

'This interview had obtained currency in English newspapers, and, of course, it was necessary to give to it a flat *dementi*. In the House of Commons, therefore, the Prime Minister read out a repudiation on the King's behalf. "His Majesty the King has had his attention directed to certain statements reporting an interview with Lord Northcliffe appearing in the *Daily Mail* and reproduced in the *Daily Express* and some of the Irish newspapers. The statements con-
o

tained in the report are a complete fabrication. No
such conversations as which are alleged took place,
nor were any such remarks as those which are alleged
made by His Majesty."

' "His Majesty also desires it to be made quite clear,
as the contrary is suggested in the interview, that in his
speech to the Parliament of North Ireland he followed
the invariable constitutional practice relating to
speeches from the Throne in Parliament." '

Sir George Arthur's own comment on the King's
statement is curious. He wrote: 'The so-called
"repudiation" was not one of the King's happiest
pronouncements and seemed to bear upon its face the
imprint of the Prime Minister's rather rough handwriting. . . .'

Now exactly what does this mean? If it has any
meaning, then surely it suggests that the King himself
did not deny the statements attributed to him, but that
the denial was put into the King's mouth by Mr Lloyd
George, which in turn suggests very strongly that the
denial was a 'diplomatic denial' and that the alleged
conversation may well have taken place. Apart from
this, Sir George Arthur affirms that Northcliffe never
enjoyed Court favour; nevertheless, Northcliffe used
to show visitors a signed photograph of Queen
Alexandra which the Queen had given him. Whether
or not Northcliffe enjoyed Court favour is, however,
beside the question in this enquiry into his statesmanlike qualities. If the denial was as suggested by Sir
George Arthur, and the fundamental facts were as
stated in the alleged interview, did Northcliffe grant
an interview during the course of which he made the
statements attributed to him?

Northcliffe sent his 'humble duty' to His Majesty
and denied the interview, but the controversy went on

and still goes on. While it is not possible to sift the evidence to arrive at a verdict which pleases everybody, it may be suggested that a member of Northcliffe's *entourage* with him in New York at the time of the interview rightly or wrongly allowed it to be understood that he was speaking on Lord Northcliffe's behalf.

But in any case, it must be stressed, on the principle that there is seldom smoke without fire, that Northcliffe's tactless intervention in a delicate Anglo-Irish situation once more proved his lack of statesmanlike qualities.

Other have reached similar conclusions through different channels. Lord Beaverbrook wrote: '. . . he had no realisation whatever of the political temperament'. Yet Lloyd George did twice offer him Cabinet rank, but was this because Lloyd George believed Northcliffe possessed statesmanlike qualities or was it because Lloyd George believed he would have some control over Northcliffe the newspaper proprietor once he was his Cabinet colleague?

With the offer of the Air Ministry portfolio I have dealt with in the chapter, 'Northcliffe Goes to War'. There remains to be told, however, the story of the second refusal.

In July 1918, Lloyd George offered Northcliffe the War Office portfolio. Northcliffe this time did not write a letter; he merely telephoned to Lloyd George's secretary, the late Sir John Davies, and declined the offer and asked him to thank Lloyd George for having made it. Northcliffe gave no reason for his refusal, but a little later his manoeuvring explained his refusal.

Northcliffe told Lord Reading (Sir Rufus Isaacs) that he did not want to be saddled with a post which meant looking after a mass of detail, but he was willing to be Minister without Portfolio, provided he was a member of the War Cabinet. Reading was requested to bring this suggestion to the attention of Lloyd George, but the Premier would have none of it.

Northcliffe returned from America during the war with the self-assurance that he was destined to be Prime Minister. His vanity had reached the megalo-maniac stage, as has already been said, and the reason for it was largely due to the applause he had received in the United States. The man who had twice rejected Cabinet rank now wanted the biggest prize of all. Here perhaps one should inject a few notes on secret history. Both Mr Lloyd George and Lord Haldane publicly poured scorn on Northcliffe's pretensions to the Premiership of Great Britain, and calm and considered judgment does lead to the conclusion that Northcliffe would have been an impossible Premier, but in 1915, when the Battle of Loos was fought and the morale of the Army in Flanders was not at its highest level, to say the least, Lloyd George and some of his closest associates toyed with the idea of asking Horatio Bottomley to form a Government; yes, Bottomley— the man who later served a term of seven years' imprisonment for heartless frauds on poor people. For many years prior to his trial Bottomley was notorious as a charlatan and swindler, but he was a fine orator, he had a wonderful brain and he could write the sort of articles which made a direct appeal to the masses. Moreover, he was a proprietor of a weekly paper, *John Bull*, which had a large circulation among soldiers and their families. Nothing, fortunately, came of this project to make Bottomley the head of a British Government, but such a plan existed. Choose then, if you must, between Bottomley and Northcliffe! What-ever may have been Northcliffe's drawbacks, they

would have been better for Britain than the qualities
Bottomley possessed.

Disappointed that he was not made Premier, Northcliffe nevertheless thought he should be one of the
British delegates to the Paris Peace Conference. Before
the war ended, there was a preliminary Inter-Allied
meeting at Versailles. Northcliffe went to Paris, a
somewhat pathetic figure. He never looked his best
in formal attire. Looking like Narcissus in a top hat,
beneath his eyes the usual peculiar look, as if grease
had been rubbed into the skin, he walked up to a
group of Anglo-American newspaper men waiting
in the lobby of the Hotel Crillon to see Lloyd George.
There was Northcliffe, the great newspaper proprietor,
and nobody bothering to ask his opinion. Clemenceau,
an ex-journalist, was Premier of France; but Northcliffe, who was he?

'I think that everything is going very well', he
volunteered.

Nobody answered. He walked away.

Northcliffe told his intimates: 'I ought to be in Paris
to keep an eye on Lloyd George; he will let us down'.
Of course, this remark was repeated to Lloyd George.
Lloyd George toyed with the idea of making Asquith
a member of the British delegation, but when he
learned that Northcliffe would oppose this idea, he
dropped it. Later he thought of putting Northcliffe in
'control of the Press at the Conference', but he dropped
that idea, too, and gave the post of British Press
Director to the proprietor of the *News of the World*, his
friend, the late Lord Riddel. Northcliffe was furious,
and this led to the final break between Northcliffe and
Lloyd George.

Northcliffe's evil genius caused him to do all he
possibly could to embarrass the Premier during the

long-drawn-out negotiations in Paris, and he organised
the sending of a telegram to the Premier by a number
of M.P.s who stated their fear that British interests in
Paris were in danger. Lloyd George made a reply in
the House of Commons. The Premier did not mention
Northcliffe by name, but the House and millions of
people knew to whom he was referring. Lloyd George
said Northcliffe was a man 'here today, jumping there
tomorrow. I would as soon trust a grasshopper.' Then
the Premier went on to say: 'When a man is labouring
under a keen sense of disappointment—however un-
justified, however ridiculous his expectations—a man
under these conditions is apt to think the world is
badly run'.

'When a man has deluded himself and all the people
whom he permits to come near him help to delude
him, into the belief that he is the only man who can
win the war, and he is waiting for the clamour of the
multitude that is going to demand his presence to
direct operations, and there is not a whisper, not a
sound, he is rather disappointed. . . . Yet nobody
comes near him to tell him so. So he publishes the
Peace Terms in advance, and he waits for the call. But
the call does not come. . . . Under these conditions I
am prepared to make allowances, but when that
diseased vanity is carried to the point of sowing
dissension between lands ("Hats off to France")
whose unity is essential to the peace and happiness of
the world, then I say that not even that kind of vanity
is a justification for so black a crime.'

Strong words, strong words indeed, words from a
man goaded by a newspaper proprietor and stung to
desperation. Words which wrote *finis* to anything and
everything Northcliffe hoped for and expected. Only
his newspapers were left to him.

Did Northcliffe get what he wanted? In his home life we must on the evidence say he was a disappointed man; as for his aspirations in the world of British statecraft, the answer must be likewise an unqualified negative; but as a man who during his lifetime made life in Britain less drab, less commonplace, who gave his millions of readers pleasant daily thrills, he must be and always should be remembered with gratitude.

THE summer breeze swayed the tree tops which separate the backs of the houses on the south side of Pall Mall from their opposite number in Carlton Gardens. In the cream-coloured house belonging to the Duke of Devonshire there had been some swiftly moving interior engineering: a lift was constructed to raise to the roof the person of the Duke's neighbour, Viscount Northcliffe, who was in the hands of four male nurses. In the intervals between lunacy and lucidity, did Northcliffe ever remember that this roof now lent to him so that he could enjoy quietness and fresh air, once capped the home of a man against whom the Chief had waged a bitter war of words? In this house there had lived Viscount Kitchener, the soldier Northcliffe had once boomed and boosted and had then sought to cast out. Now workmen were finishing their all-night task of completing a wooden hut, and into this hut they brought a bed and on this bed there now lay the bulging body of the man for whom millions toiled, upon whose smile or frown the happiness of the homes of thousands depended. This then was the end of a long Odyssey. But how was it the Chief came to be in such a state of mental and physical collapse?

Northcliffe set out on his much-heralded world tour

in July 1921; it was to be a tour to thrill the world. A few hours after his departure he began to bombard Carmelite House, Fleet Street, with strange despatches. For instance, the Chief sent to the *Daily Mail* the full shipboard menus—first, second, and third class; he demanded they should be published and they were published. At this time it was rumoured that Northcliffe was suffering from general paralysis of the insane, but it was also given out that he was suffering from a rare form of heart disease.

When Northcliffe reached New York, the city was in the midst of an awful heatwave. At that time a former leading roving correspondent of the *Daily Mail* was there, on the staff of a New York morning newspaper. This man, until he was dismissed, had been one of Northcliffe's favourites. When he saw his former Chief, he was appalled. Northcliffe was working at full steam, like an over-wound clock; he seemed on the verge of a breakdown. With Northcliffe was Mr Wickham Steed, of *The Times*, who acted as the Chief's spokesman and liaison officer with the American Press; any editor had only to ask, and Mr Steed obliged with Northcliffe's opinion on any subject, but particularly on Ireland, a country about which he made some very curious pronouncements.

A member of the *Daily Mail* reporting staff, the late John Prioleau, was also present; his job was to write Northcliffe's impressions of New York. The fact that Prioleau was paying his first visit to the United States made no difference.

Mr Steed was editing *The Times* from a distance of three thousand miles; the Editor's headquarters were in the Gotham Hotel, West 54th Street, New York City, and at his elbow was his proprietor, Northcliffe, showing distressing signs of a mental malady.

It was at this moment that the late Lord Curzon, British Foreign Secretary, still smarting from the hurt Northcliffe had inflicted on this vain and pompous person by saying that his real name was Cohen, sent a dispatch to the British Ambassador at Washington, saying that Northcliffe was not paying an official visit to the United States and that the White House was to be informed accordingly.

Lord Northcliffe was playing the role of Pooh-Bah in a heat-ridden New York during the 'Silly Season'. He announced to all and sundry that he was ready to answer any questions anybody liked to put to him. The thermometer registered ninety degrees in the shade. The Chief's suite on the twelfth floor of the hotel was jammed with people who for three days came to seek pearls of wisdom from the lips of a panting perspiring man who sat on a platform wearing a sweat-soaked tropical suit; every two hours he would call a halt, retire to his dressing-room to change his clothes and swallow a tumblerful of champagne; then back to the platform to face a barrage of inane questions, while grouped in the background were American reporters and press photographers.

The questions ranged from queries as to Northcliffe's opinions on chewing-gum, films and women's stockings, to the character of the Prince of Wales, but numbers of people, men and women, came hoping they would be able to obtain some personal benefit. Thus came beggars and bounders; film publicity people trying to climb on the Northcliffe band-waggon; delegations hoping for contributions; and New York East Side inventors.

For three days this continued, because, short of 'copy' in the 'Silly Season', reporters saw possibilities in making fun of this once-great man. Thus if there was

a shortage of callers, a reporter would go down into
the street and make a deal with a passer-by—the cash
value of ten dollars—to go up to the twelfth floor and
ask Northcliffe a question. Some pretty queer questions
there were, too. One reporter briefed a young girl to
go upstairs and quiz Northcliffe about his opinions on
Free Love. He gave them, too, and they were, of
course, duly reported in the New York newspapers.

Northcliffe was suffering badly from insomnia.
After these foolish days of stupid questions, when
Northcliffe brusquely brushed aside all attempts to
have him put an end to them, he would have himself
driven for four or five hours at top speed along the
roads of Long Island.

Undoubtedly, this tortured, restless genius often
tried to find peace in being driven at night, this poor-
rich man, trying to do the impossible: to escape from
himself. One of the most pathetic mental pictures I
have of him dates to the spring before his death, when
he was being driven by his faithful chauffeur, Pine,
from Pau to Paris. He was being driven by night
through the Forest of Fontainebleau, and suddenly, for
a very brief spell, peace came to him: the heavy cloak
that enshrouded his powerful personality fell from him
and he became quietened and gentle in speech and
watched the rabbits scuttle across the beams of the
headlights of the car.

The tour continued and Northcliffe's mental malady
became worse. The late Lord Asquith wrote in his
memoirs that Northcliffe cabled King George V,
saying: 'I am turning Roman Catholic', and the King
replied: 'I cannot help it'.

Back in Britain in February 1922, it was not long
before Northcliffe became the object of Fleet Street
rumours: 'Northcliffe is going mad'; yet he continued

to control his publications. But less than a month after
his return, he was off again, this time to Pau, where
took place the curious *Times* conversations concerning
the lowering of the selling price of the newspaper, to
which reference has been made.

A few months after the visit to Pau, Northcliffe
went to stay at the Hotel Eden, Cap d'Ail,
on the French Riviera. Here he was visited by the
same ex-favourite who had last seen him in New York
during the world tour. The reporter had become
Paris correspondent of the now defunct New York
World, and wished to interview Northcliffe about his
visit to the Far East.

The reporter was terribly shocked in the change in
the physical appearance of Northcliffe; there was a
wild look now in his eyes; his flesh was sagging; his
voice was hoarse, his face flushed, and he lay in bed
and appeared very weak.

Northcliffe said he felt very ill and doubted whether
he would even leave the hotel alive. Then he became
querulous. He said to the visitor: 'What do you think
of these people in the hotel to worry me like this?
Last night I had cold chicken and a bottle of Chablis
and this morning at lunch when I called for what was
left over, they said I had eaten it all. I know I did not.'

At this time, like puffs of an evil wind, fits of madness
swept over him. The local representative of a world-
famed British motor car came to call on Northcliffe
at his request. The man was wearing white kid gloves,
which infuriated Northcliffe, who telephoned to the
headquarters of the company to demand that their
representative be 'sacked', and, to appease Northcliffe,
the firm went through the motions of dismissing the
man.

Northcliffe returned to Britain and none of the men

in close touch with him seemed to think anything was wrong. In May 1922, he talked about returning in three or four years' time. In passing he affirmed that 'the Germans' were buying shares in the *Daily Mail* and he could not stop them. He then gave out a story to his office executives that he was going to Holland, but most of them knew he intended going to Germany. The reason for his departure from Britain he himself attributed to the forthcoming visit to London of the late William Randolph Hearst and Mrs Hearst. Northcliffe said it had been announced in the United States that he was going to present Mrs Hearst at Court, and that the man who made this announcement must be mad! He made other rambling statements and gave instructions that no cartoons making Lloyd George appear genial were to be published; Carmelite House Lloyd George cartoons were to be modelled on those appearing in the French newspapers. Just on the eve of departure Northcliffe made an attack on office nepotism; the man who had placed his brothers in key positions ordained that a man was to be given the job of clearing out relations of members of the staff. Finally he gave orders that even if Seymour Hicks protested at the daily praise of his play, *The Man in Dress Clothes*, and asked that they should cease, the protests were to be ignored.

Northcliffe now (May 1922) conceived the last 'mystery story' of his life. He pretended that at great personal risk and peril he would go into Germany and there he would write a series of all-revealing articles about the secret soul of the country. He demanded that his stories should be 'played up' in *The Times* and *Daily Mail*. He took the name of Leonard Brown. This is how the late Lord D'Abernon, then British Ambassador at Berlin, related the visit.

'During three days' stay in Cologne, Northcliffe only went once beyond the garden of the house where he was staying. His only visitor was an itinerant correspondent. All Northcliffe wrote about his adventures between the frontier and Cologne was purely imaginary. Northcliffe had nothing but a straight drive along the main road and spoke to nobody.'

Yet out of this brief journey into Germany, Northcliffe concocted the wildest farrago of nonsense imaginable. Some of his articles appeared in *The Times* and the *Daily Mail*. Then some hidden hand stopped them. It was none too soon.

On arrival at the Belgian frontier—he was travelling by car—he decided he had been poisoned; 'they saw me before I saw them', he declared. He said he had been given some poisoned ice-cream; the 'yes-men' supported this contention: but Northcliffe changed his mind and declared he had not been poisoned. But he continued to pretend—as he had done for many years—that his life was in danger by assassination. He sent what he called 'a secret messenger' (actually he was a hired courier) to Cologne 'to make the necessary arrangements'. He said the man would be recognised by his grey hat. It must be remembered that all this occurred in June 1922, two years after peace with Germany had been signed, and Northcliffe, who merely spent a few hours in Cologne, in the British Zone of Occupied Germany, pretended to himself and his readers that he was taking great risks and running grave dangers. 'I'm not afraid for my life', he declared, 'I shoot from the hip.' He was at that time carrying an automatic revolver, which was fortunately taken from him.

In the twilight period of Northcliffe's life, revolvers played a very curious part. In Switzerland, a little prior to the Sunday afternoon when he was certified insane, Wickham Steed found him in bed, brandishing a revolver at his dressing-gown hanging behind the door. Northcliffe declared it was an intruder trying to assassinate him. In his book *Men and Power*, Lord Beaverbrook, on the authority of the late Sir Thomas Horder, relates yet another revolver story.

When Lord Northcliffe lay dying on the roof of the house in Carlton Gardens, Lord Horder was called in for a consultation. As he entered the room, Northcliffe looked at him and exclaimed: 'Another of Lloyd George's bloody knights!' He drew a revolver from beneath his pillow and pointed it at Horder. A male nurse knocked up his patient's arm and presumably saved Lord Horder's life. Lord Beaverbrook's dramatic comment was: 'Lord Horder lived; Northcliffe died'.

When his motor car was nearing Cologne, some explosions were heard in the distance. It was the Allied Military Control Commission at work, blowing up some forts. Northcliffe, who on many occasions had declared that he was 'a war casualty'—and the 'yes-men' agreed—now exclaimed as he heard the explosions: 'As I expected, the Germans are attacking.'

The articles showed a coarse and clumsy lasciviousness; Northcliffe declared that the most outstanding feature of the German landscape was the number of pregnant women, and he also described the legs of German women, which he said were the ugliest in the world.

The disastrous trip ended, Northcliffe went to Paris, from whence he sent one of his famous *communiqués* to Carmelite House. He mentioned his German visit, his mysterious illness, and then continued as follows: 'I wish this *communiqué* to be prominently posted in a hundred different rooms, because Mr Price, my private secretary, who is doing important work of

which Carmelite House does not know, is being
hounded to death by certain people in the office, most
of them enormously paid.'

'There's an idea that Mr Price knows my views.
He does not know my views and many mistakes occur
through asking him. Any person who in future asks
Mr Price any question whatever will incur my grave
displeasure.'

'As for my whereabouts, Mr Price rarely knows.
When I am abroad, it is known only to my family. I
hope I shall not have to say this again. The telephone
people have orders to keep a list of those who try to
get through to Mr Price. A list is being kept of all
such calls and I'll see this list on my return, which
will be very shortly.' Actually, he never did return
either to Carmelite House or Printing House Square.

From Paris Northcliffe went to Boulogne and booked
himself a small bedroom. His Paris office had passed
on to London his demand that a secretary should be
sent him immediately. *The Times* sent an ex-bank clerk
with a board school education, a man named Douglas
Reed, with a good war record. He was at this time a
telephonist in *The Times* London office, but was later
a member of the Foreign staff. Northcliffe was most
annoyed that *The Times* should have sent *him* anyone
with such an educational record.

Reed has a fantastic tale to tell of the few days he
spent with Northcliffe before he was dismissed. Northcliffe was still masquerading as Leonard Brown and
kept under his pillow a black silk bag which he claimed
a man had left at the hotel for 'Mr Brown'. He called
Reed's attention to the colour, black, which he
explained was the colour of Death. Daily Northcliffe
sent cables to *The Times*, to the *Daily Mail* and the
Evening News. As a result of some of the abuse he heaped

NORTHCLIFFE

MDCCCLXV

MCMXXII

*Bust of Lord Northcliffe outside the church of St Dunstan's-in-the-West,
Fleet Street*

on their heads, two directors of the *Daily Mail*, the late Sir Andrew Caird and the late Mr W. G. Fish, issued writs for libel against Lord Northcliffe, but withdrew them when he was dying. Reed states: 'To one eminent journalist, we telegraphed: "You are fired"; to another: "Hear you have been seen walking down Fleet Street in a top hat. Don't do it"; we wrote long letters ... in which we discussed in satirical vein all manner of things, from the skinny shanks of a famous lady to the Jewish influence in English life.'

Reed's career with Lord Northcliffe was not a gay one; true, the Chief put his salary up to £500 a year —a way he had—and also presented him with £150 and told him to go to London and buy a suitcase. Reed purchased articles of urgent need and returned to Boulogne minus the suitcase. He was 'fired' by the Chief, who told him contemptuously that he could keep the £150, because he would never earn enough to repay it!

Northcliffe's last words to Reed before he left for Paris were: 'Goodbye. You will never see me again in this world.'

Northcliffe went to Switzerland, where he had attacks of violence. Mr Wickham Steed, Editor of *The Times*, Mr Peter Goudie, then Editor of the Paris *Daily Mail*, accompanied by the late Leicester Harmsworth (a brother) and two male nurses, went to Switzerland to bring him back. He had to be placed in a strait-jacket.

The *History of The Times* has this to say about the matter:

'During the evening of Monday, June 12, Hudson (Sir Robert Hudson), Treves (Sir Frederick Treves) and Steed (H. Wickham Steed) consulted. From Lausanne Treves summoned a brilliant French nerve

P

specialist holding British medical degrees, who arrived
later with a trained nurse and a medical attendant.
He certified Northcliffe as insane. They all passed the
night close to the patient's room. As the night progressed an increasingly serious view of the case was
taken by Treves, and Hudson wired home for Dr
Seymour Price. A serious view was also being taken
in London. During Tuesday, as the result of telegrams
that Northcliffe got his valet to despatch, action was
taken at Printing House Square and at Carmelite
House. It was not what the Chief intended. Steed had
given strict instructions to Harold Snoad, Northcliffe's
secretary, to send no telegram without referring to
him; but as the Chief sent Snoad to the post office
with a few harmless telegrams which Steed had passed,
Steed feared that Northcliffe would bribe a waiter or
a nurse to send some other telegrams without his
knowledge.'

All possible precautions were taken to keep the
news out of the newspapers. The help of M. Poincaré,
then Premier of France, was invoked. M. Poincaré
offered the use of his own motor car, but finally a
special train was chartered. The Paris correspondent
of the Exchange Telegraph Company sent a story
saying that Lord Northcliffe, accompanied by two male
nurses, had passed through Paris.

The destination was Boulogne again, the same hotel,
the Cristol Hotel, where Northcliffe had negotiated
the purchase of *The Times*. Here a whole floor was
reserved for the maniacal millionaire. Like many men
when the madness is on them, Northcliffe when seized
with these attacks had tremendous strength. He broke
away from his keepers and walked about the hotel in
a condition of stark nakedness. The other visitors
were asked to leave; the Northcliffe party took over

the whole hotel, where Northcliffe did great damage, smashing mirrors, crockery and glasses. Finally, when he was taken to London, the Paris manager of *The Times* was sent to Boulogne to 'clear up the mess', as he expressed it.

The Odyssey ends. Here then is Northcliffe back in London, the city where he built his fortune and the fortune of many others. He was mad, but there were moments of sanity, when the present came back with a rush and he wanted to return to his affairs.

On June 18, 1922, Mr Thomas Marlowe, the Editor of the *Daily Mail*, said to Mr Tom Clarke, the News Editor: 'He (Northcliffe) has got to be kept away from the telephone. . . . If he rings you up— listen to him, don't argue, be happy in your conversation with him. Agree with all he says. Take down any instructions he gives you.' Late that Sunday evening an assistant said to Clarke: 'Someone rang you up a moment ago'.

'Who?' enquired Clarke.

'It sounded like the Chief', answered the assistant. 'He said "Tom", and when I said you were out of the room, he switched off.'

All the telephones Northcliffe could reach, so they thought, had been cut, but he found one in his wife's room. The following day, Northcliffe telephoned several times to one or two people. Clarke reported: 'He speaks in a whisper—a ghostly voice. He says he hears that people say he is mad. "They are watching me".'

'They decided that Northcliffe might break loose and somehow find his way to Carmelite House, so his private telephone line was restored, but when he did come through on the telephone, only two members of the staff, one managerial and one editorial, were allowed to receive his communications.

On Thursday, June 20, the *Daily Mail* announced that Lord Northcliffe had returned from the Continent and was receiving treatment for weakness of the heart, accentuated by ptomaine poisoning. The *Daily Mail* set up the proprietor's obituary in type, but the Chief was now full of morphia and there were no more telephone calls.

Meanwhile, in the hut on the roof there were strange happenings which can best be related in documentary evidence. It evidently occurred to several people that a very large amount of money was at stake. Was the figure on the bed that of a man capable of disposing of his vast wealth? We have seen how, having learned that 'they' thought him mad, Northcliffe demanded in a ghostly whisper over the telephone that 'the best reporter be sent to get the story'. But what was actually happening in Carlton Gardens, London? Mr Leslie S. Richardson, one of the male nurses in attendance on the Chief, after Northcliffe's death made an affidavit as follows:

'In the matter of the estate of the Right Honourable Alfred Charles William Viscount Northcliffe, deceased.

'I, Leslie S. Richardson, Male Nurse, of 54, Beaumont Street, W.1, make Oath and say as follows:

'On or about July 1st, 1922, I was engaged by Mr Price as Nurse Attendant to go to No. 1 Carlton Gardens, London, S.W. Another institution had been written to, but they were short of staff, and when they rang through to us I was sent. I went into the sitting-room at No. 1 Carlton Gardens, and sat there for about an hour. I had not then the least idea whose house it was. I had been there some time when one of the footmen just happened to say, rather flurriedly, "I shall be glad when Lord Northcliffe gets better".

After a time I was taken upstairs; there were two or three men there. I was never really told what was wrong with Lord Northcliffe, but I was told not to divulge what I heard there. I was sworn to secrecy. I had been there a day or two before I actually saw Lord Northcliffe. One of the other men introduced me to his lordship when he shook hands with me. His lordship was half in and half out of bed. He said he hoped we would get on together. After that we nurses used to take it in turns to sit with him, one inside and one outside his room. He gave me the impression of a man who was *non compos mentis*. He was always talking about business affairs and sometimes when I was sitting with him he would say: "My young man, I am going to give you £1,000 a year and a hen farm". That was his way of talking. This sort of thing went on for some days, when he suddenly said, "I am going to write a fresh will". We took no notice, but we used to give him paper and pencil just to pacify him, and he used to sit and write. He was not allowed anything to read, nor to see any newspapers. He was continually giving us notes to take to the City, *The Times* office, etc. Sometimes we would tear them up and sometimes we kept them. We had to do this to pacify him. He used to write on strips of paper and we would say, "Certainly, my lord, we will take it", and think no more about it.

'He made this will in his own handwriting and he asked one or two of us to sign it. I said, "Certainly", not dreaming for a moment that there was anything valid about it. It was just to pacify a man who was sick. There was not any question of its being properly witnessed or put forward as a proper will. He simply asked me to sign it and I signed it. No one witnessed my signature. I remember this particular instance, because instead of taking the thing and putting it away, it was left about in his room and read by other parties. This paper, as signed by me, was left lying on a huge table on which medical things, lunch, etc. were put.

'I remember Dr Seymour Price coming in with one of the other surgeons and he picked it up. He said, "This is important", and I thought: "Oh dear, we might have destroyed it". I never bothered any more about it at the time or saw it again.

'I stayed on for a time until after the funeral. I went to Albemarle Street by request. They asked me for a statement. I told them the same as I have stated in this affidavit. They knew it was not a valid will. I explained to these people that I did not want to be dragged into anything, but I was stating facts. I just emphasised the fact that I only signed it to pacify Lord Northcliffe, or words to that effect, and I am sure his lordship was not really conscious of what he was doing. That was why he had so many attendants with him, though it was not necessary at all times. His lordship was worth plenty of money, so it was not a matter of expense. There were many medical men attending him also. I remember Sir Thomas Horder, Dr Seymour Price and Dr Drake, and a young doctor who came, but left after a time, when another doctor came. They ordered all telephones to be cut off from his lordship. I do not doubt for a moment that the bringing forward of this will was wrong, as nothing written by a patient in his lordship's state could be taken seriously. I did not read the will and I did not witness it in the presence of a third party. His lordship would bring out papers by his bedside and would say: "Look here, young man, I want you to put your name to this". I have many papers he had written and I saved a few to keep his handwriting as a souvenir, but most of them were destroyed as valueless. I was the last one with him when he died, giving him oxygen at the end.'

Another male nurse, Mr Charles Printall, made an affidavit as follows:

'In the matter of the estate of the Right Honourable Alfred Charles William, Viscount Northcliffe, deceased.

'I, Charles Richard Printall, of 5 Mornington Terrace, Newham-on-Severn, in the County of Gloucestershire, make Oath and say as follows:

'On or about the 1st July One thousand nine hundred and twenty-two, I was engaged as a Nurse Attendant to go to No. 1 Carlton Gardens, London, S.W.1. I was sworn to secrecy.

'I remember putting my name to paper—whether it was written by Lord Northcliffe or myself I cannot remember at this time, I signed my name to it at his lordship's request; we were alone at the time.

'Some time after his lordship's death, Mr William Graham of the firm of Messrs. Nicholson, Graham & Co., 19/21 Moorgate, E.C., sent for me and questioned me on this paper which I had signed at Lord Northcliffe's request, when I told him I attached no importance to it as a will, for it had not been properly witnessed.

CHAS. R. PRINTALL.'

Another male nurse, Mr John Howden, made the following affidavit:

'In the matter of the Estate of the Right Honourable Alfred Charles William Viscount Northcliffe, deceased.

'I, John Daniel Howden, of 54 Beaumont Street,

London, W.1, in the county of London, W., Male
Nurse, make Oath and say as follows:

'1. On or about the 22nd of July, one thousand
nine hundred and twenty-two, I was employed at No.
1 Carlton Gardens, London W., as a Male Nurse to
attend on the late Viscount Northcliffe.

'2. While Dr Ernest Drake was in attendance on
Viscount Northcliffe, he—Dr Drake—called me in
from the adjoining room into his lordship's bedroom
on or about July 22nd, 1922, when the doctor requested
me to sign my name to a document which he called
a will.

'3. I did not see the clause relative to witnesses'
signature, which I have since read in a copy of the
will. When I signed the paper only Lord Northcliffe
and Dr Drake and myself were in the room. I did not
see Dr Drake sign his name to the document. I did
not see Lord Northcliffe sign this or any document
while I was in his bedroom at that time, for had he
written the words "Alfred Charles William Harmsworth" I should have made a remark about it,
knowing his name was Lord Northcliffe as that was
how we always addressed his lordship. It never
occurred to me that the document I signed would be
put forward as a valid will, owing to the state of Lord
Northcliffe's mind, otherwise I should have come
forward before now and given the above information.

'4. Within a few days of Lord Northcliffe's funeral,
I was requested to call at Mr William Graham's
office of the firm of Messrs Nicholson Graham and
Jones, 19/21 Moorgate, E.C.2, when I was questioned
by Mr Graham as to the condition of Lord Northcliffe's mind when the document I was asked to sign
by Dr Drake was signed by me. To the best of my
belief I had previously seen Mr Graham at his lord-

ship's house, 1 Carlton Gardens. Mr Graham wanted me to give a statement in case there was an enquiry about Lord Northcliffe's affairs. I told him that Lord Northcliffe was mentally afflicted. Mr Graham paid me One Guinea and I left. I refused to sign any statement.

'5. Some considerable time afterwards, whilst I was nursing the Hon. Basil Fitzherbert at Greyshott, Hindhead, a gentleman who told me he was a solicitor, called in a Rolls-Royce car about four o'clock one afternoon. He endeavoured to get a statement from me concerning Lord Northcliffe. I refused and informed him that I had already told another solicitor my opinion as to the state of Lord Northcliffe's mind. He then became very insistent that I should consent to sign a statement prepared by him. I refused and he was very annoyed and said: "Won't you help us in this way?" I said "No, I will sign nothing; if you want me you can subpoena me in the usual way. I have nothing more to say and I think you had better leave."

                    JOHN DANIEL HOWDEN, Male Nurse,
                          54 Beaumont Street, London, W.1.'

It seems that the document called the will and signed by Mr Printall and Mr Richardson was written in pencil and reads as follows:

'My last Will and Testament, Alfred Viscount Northcliffe. My entire possessions in Europe and North America, my newspapers, including *The Times* and the largest paper-making industry in the world, which includes Gravesend and Grand Falls, to be at once given to my wife under the assistance of Sir Robert Hudson.

'I, Alfred Charles William Viscount Northcliffe, being in good mental state, though suffering from one

dangerous disease, Indian Jungle fever, and another
unknown to any doctors in Great Britain, poisoning
by ice-cream supplied on the Belgian Frontier, where
I was unfortunately known first, I bequeath everything I possess to my wife to use exactly as she chooses
under Sir Robert Hudson's guidance. She will give
for her use £10,000 per annum to my darling
mother. She will, I know, never neglect her
workpeople, with whom since 1888, when we began,
we have never had a strike, except an American
strike, which our Newfoundland workers detested and
broke away from. I particularly desire that my
darling wife should re-marry if she wishes. She and I
both know who we desire she should marry, and it
would help her in a life that is more like a queen than
an ordinary person. Next in order to my wife in
importance to this will is my sister Mrs Christabel
Burton. Although the poorest member of our family,
she from the outset resisted with energy and vigour
and counteraction the efforts of the foolish members
of the Harmsworth family to wreak their vengeance
on one who has built things up by originality. The
fortunes these men have made, with the exception of
Lord Rothermere, who is a first-rate financier, are
purely imitated. I invented the *Daily Mirror*. It was a
failure at first, and Rothermere ran for his life. When
it became a success, I sold it to him for nothing,
because I had more troublesome work in hand—
reconstruction of *The Times*, heavy work at Newfoundland, in which my darling wife always accompanied me, the only woman of the family who ever
raised a finger in this business. I wish whatever seems
suitable to be given to my niece, Sheila. I wish
Mother's maid Edith to have a life pension of £100
per annum, Enid Stokes to be well provided for. I

commit my soul to God. I sign this will which revokes all others.

NORTHCLIFFE
Seventh July 1922.

Chas. R. Printall, Newham Close
Leslie S. Richardson.'

The aforementioned will was held to be invalid, and, later, another will was placed on the Somerset House file.

That is the document which brought so much money into the coffers of the lawyers when it was contested in the Law Courts. The third codicil to this valid and, therefore, legal will was signed in April, 1922, four months before Northcliffe died. At that time many curious things were happening. There was, for instance, the remarkable appointment, already mentioned in this book, of the commissionaire of Carmelite House, Glover, to be censor of *Daily Mail* advertisements. Northcliffe rang the News Editor on the telephone to tell him of the appointment. This News Editor recorded: 'With an uncomfortable thought that he might one day appoint the office-boy as censor of news, I said he must be joking. "You won't really do that, Chief, will you?" I asked.

' "Why not? Of course I will . . . Someone has been saying I am off my head. Not you, is it?" ' This conversation took place a few days before the third codicil was signed. A few days after the signature—May 3—Mr Tom Clarke recorded: 'How long will the Chief last?' A few days later Northcliffe complained that Lloyd George was under the thumb of 'propaganding Jews'. 'Don't be led by the Scots or the Jews', he told Clarke.

Now Northcliffe was a dying man rumours got about, despite all the secrecy, and people began to call at Carmelite House with offers of 'cures'. Northcliffe knew he was dying, and asked the Editors of *The Times* and *Daily Mail* to give his death a page in each newspaper. The *Daily Mail*, ten days before he died, began to 'make up' the page.

On Monday morning, August 14, 1922, Alfred Charles William Harmsworth, first Viscount Northcliffe, died at the age of fifty-seven years, one month and one day. The official cause of his death was stated to be infective or ulcerative endocarditis, which might have been set up by the condition of his teeth, but actually the cause was never known. It was known, however, that this poison had entered the blood stream. Northcliffe had often stated that he had heart disease, but the condition of his heart when he died showed no sign of disease, except that his heart had been affected by the poisoned blood stream, a condition, however, that had not existed longer than a few months. Northcliffe never made any secret of his maladies; he had had that minor operation on his throat; he had had eye trouble, and, in his youth, pneumonia. His grave mental storms, which, as we have seen, grew worse as he grew older, were symptomatic of another malady, but we also find, as has been recorded, Northcliffe making semi-serious references to his reported madness.

When Northcliffe died on his neighbour's roof in Carlton Gardens, most of the members of his family were present, including Lady Northcliffe. News of the Chief's death was quickly known in Fleet Street; reporters and photographers hurried to Carlton Gardens. About two hours after her husband died, Lady Northcliffe left the house. She was immediately

'snapped' by the press photographers. Lady Northcliffe was extremely annoyed, not realising that she
was a victim of a branch of enterprise particularly
developed by her husband.

A few months after her husband's death, the newspapers announced her marriage to Sir Robert Hudson,
the gentleman mentioned in the invalid Northcliffe
will.

For many years, Northcliffe had been but a rather
dimmed figure of legend, but as soon as he died,
London flocked to his funeral. This occurs not more
often than once in each generation of Londoners. A
man is forgotten; people do not really know whether
he is dead or still lives; then his death is announced
and London recalls the magic of far-off forgotten
things. Before the Northcliffe funeral, London had
never witnessed such a sight since the funeral of 'Roger
Tichborne', the notorious 'claimant'. He died in a
Paddington slum, but what a funeral he had! Now
Northcliffe lay dead, and London suddenly remembered not Northcliffe, but 'young Alfred Harmsworth',
the man who had brought drama and romance and
colour into their drab lives, and they flocked to pay
him respect.

Northcliffe was buried on Thursday, August 17,
1922. There was a service at Westminster Abbey; in
Northcliffe's coffin was a little book, *Daily Light on the
Daily Path*, which his mother, who survived him, had
given him. He is buried in St Marylebone Cemetery.
The funeral procession travelled seven miles; there
were people everywhere. The Abbey had been
crowded. Lady Northcliffe received hundreds of telegrams from foreign crowned heads and presidents.
Among those who sent a message of condolence was
King George V, who could not abide Northcliffe ever

since the time of the *contretemps* in New York over the Irish question.

What a 'talking point' Lord Northcliffe would have made of that!

INDEX

BRITISH CASUALTIES
104,000
(OFFICIAL)

Evening News

Daily Mail

HAMILTON FYFE CAUGHT BY UHLANS

GREAT WATERPLANE RACE
MR. HAWKER FLIES 390 MILES in 7 HOURS

Evening News

Daily Mail

L. G.
M. G.